God in My Life

2

Rita Kay Crowder Roberts

TEACH Services, Inc.
P U B L I S H I N G
www.TEACHServices.com • (800) 367-1844

World rights reserved. This book or any portion thereof may not be copied or reproduced in any form or manner whatever, except as provided by law, without the written permission of the publisher, except by a reviewer who may quote brief passages in a review.

The author assumes full responsibility for the accuracy of all facts and quotations as cited in this book. The opinions expressed in this book are the author's personal views and interpretations, and do not necessarily reflect those of the publisher.

This book is provided with the understanding that the publisher is not engaged in giving spiritual, legal, medical, or other professional advice. If authoritative advice is needed, the reader should seek the counsel of a competent professional. All Bible references are taken from the King James Version (KJV) of the Bible. Public domain.

Copyright © 2019 Rita Kay Crowder Roberts
Copyright © 2019 TEACH Services, Inc.
ISBN-13: 978-1-4796-1104-1 (Paperback)
ISBN-13: 978-1-4796-1105-8 (ePub)
Library of Congress Control Number: 2019915073

Dedication

I bow humbly before God, my Heavenly Father, thanking Him for being in my life, allowing me to be a part of these wonderful miracles, and to share these stories to glorify Him. I also thank Him for making the many blessings out of the tragedies. Without His hand of grace, I would not be alive to write this book. He is so *awesome!*

"That I may publish with the voice of thanksgiving, and tell of all thy wondrous works" (Ps. 26:7).

A Word of Thanks to …

Penney Morton Smith

Dallas and Susanna Roberts

Atushi and Katy Roberts Yamamuro

Rachel Roberts Fourie

… and to everyone who donated help and information, and for all of their time, work, encouragement, and help in attaining.

Table of Contents

Prologue ix
Driving at Age Four 1
The Toe 3
Mouth of Babes 6
Physical Meltdown 8
Sharing 11
The Waitress 13
Strawberry Vines 14
The Bath Bee 19
God's Leading 21
The "Mean" Girl 25
Big Miracles, Few Words 28
My Friend Mildred 30
Mia 36
Bulgaria 38
The "Angel" in White 47
Thoughts 51
Life After Cancer Cure 53
Beetle Load 57
Only One Hand 58
The Shoes 60
All in Two Weeks 61
The Airplane Delay 65

Heart Attack	68
The Wad	73
Trenton Luke	75
Bus "Wreck"	78
My Daddy	82
Coral Cliffs Calamity	87
Power of Prayer Protection	89
Interview with Dr. Steve Im—Ultimate Cancer Cure	91
Miracles Back to Back	99
A Progressive Thought	101
Epilogue	105

Prologue

I am so thankful that God has always been in my life. It was obvious that He was in my life when things were going smoothly, but I realize now that even when I messed up, He was in my life, helping to straighten things out.

My friend Bea and I used to walk every morning up into the woods to "our rock." It was big enough for both of us to sit on comfortably beside each other and talk and pray together. My favorite expression was always "that's awesome." I always used it for anything and everything that I thought was super great.

One day, Bea, who was my elder in age, said to me, "'Awesome' is the best word we have in the English language, so we need to save that for anything to do with God—for respect and honor for Him alone."

She's right, of course. So I had to practice NOT using it for other things, and save it for God only.

Driving at Age Four

Well, not exactly! However, after having watched Daddy several times start the car and do the gear thing, I decided one pretty day while we were living in the outskirts of Chicago, Illinois, to take the car somewhere by myself. I have no idea where I was going or what I was thinking. But, I got into the front seat of our 1950s black coupe (obviously when no one was looking). I stood up holding onto the steering wheel, backed the car down the driveway, and into the road, before my parents could run out and catch me! Mother told me later that somehow I had put the car into reverse. By God's grace there were no cars going by on the road at that moment. Angels were taking care of this small, but adventuresome, child.

A couple of years later, when I was six, Daddy decided to go ahead and start teaching me how to drive. Things were very different back then! By now, we had a brand new '54 Chevrolet. Daddy held me on his lap and taught me how to steer the car. Every time he had some free time, he would take me "driving" on the sandy back roads in Florida in the winter and the mountainous back roads of western North Carolina in the summer, so I could learn how to steer. Then, as I got the "hang" of that, he started teaching me the gear shift. Everything back then seemed to be "stick shift."

I remember one day when Daddy said, "You're too big to sit on my lap. You sit in the driver's seat." I was so excited! But I was too short to see over the steering wheel, so I looked through between the steering wheel and the dashboard. Also, my legs didn't begin to reach the pedals, so Daddy sat beside me on the bench seat and worked the pedals with his feet.

I remember the day I could actually see *over* the steering wheel. Soon after that, my feet could reach the pedals. Now came the task of learning how to synchronize the clutch and the gear shift. Oh my! So, away we went: start, go, stall … start, go, stall … start, go, stall … start, go, stall … inching our way along the various back roads. Thankfully, God was in that, too, keeping other cars from hitting us, but even more, keeping ME from hitting other cars, the railing, animals, or the ditch, or whatever else was out there.

I'm so thankful for Daddy's patience—but mostly for God's patience. Just like my first few years of driving were filled with starts and stalls, my life was, also. Now that I'm on the "other end" of life, and looking back, I see that God was so very patient with me, like He wants all of us to be with each other, and He wants us to possess these traits, as He tells us in the following verse:

"But the fruit of the Spirit is love, joy, peace, *longsuffering*, gentleness, goodness, faith, Meekness, temperance: against such there is no law" (Gal. 5:22, 23, emphasis added).

The Toe

We had a two-seated, rocking loveseat in our living room that I adored! It was so much easier to rock both my children at the same time! Dallas had just turned six and Katy was almost one. As I sat on one side of the loveseat with a pillow in my lap, Dallas would put his head on the pillow and his body and legs across the rest of the seat. I held Katy in one arm above his head, nursing her, and my other arm across Dallas to keep him from rolling off the seat as we rocked. I would rock both of them while singing them to sleep. We all enjoyed it so much.

I could lay my head back on that loveseat and relax, too, while my feet and legs kept us rocking. Sometimes when I'd go to sleep before they did, I would wake up to, "Mommy, sing. Mommy, SING!" This one night, the rocking had ceased and all three of us had gone to sleep. I awoke and looked at my watch—it was 10:00! We had been there for over three hours, sleeping peacefully!

Now, my dilemma was to sneak out from under Dallas' head and carry Katy to her crib, then to come back and carry Dallas to bed, without awakening either of them. I managed to slide out from under his head and was walking softly across the totally dark room, carrying baby Katy, when I stubbed my little toe on an out-of-place chair. The pain was excruciating, but I managed to maintain silence till I got to Katy's crib. Then I realized that I was fainting from the pain! I had Katy over her crib, lowering her down toward the actual mattress, and at about three inches from it, I let go of her to keep from taking her with me to the floor. The short fall onto the soft mattress woke her up and she started crying. That woke up Dallas back in the living room, and he came down the hall in the dark to see what was going on.

By then Katy was standing up in her crib, screaming, because she couldn't see anything in the dark and it was scary to her, and I was lying on the floor regaining consciousness. I said, "Dallas, turn on the light," which he did. I held my throbbing left foot up to see why it was throbbing.

And there was the little toe, totally broken, and pointing in the wrong direction!

Dallas picked Katy up out of her crib and stood her on the floor, which helped her to quit crying. I propped my foot up on the side of my bed to elevate it. Dallas brought a cold washcloth to put on my head to help me revive. Every little bit he would bend over me there on the floor and turn the folded washcloth over to the cooler side. I knew something had to be done soon to get my toe back in place. We had no phone at the time. The closest house was that of my aunt and uncle, about an eighth of a mile up the road. Additionally, that very day, we had killed a copperhead snake in the road between the two houses. It was still lying there.

> *Katy was standing up in her crib, screaming, because she couldn't see anything in the dark and it was scary to her, and I was lying on the floor regaining consciousness*

I asked Dallas, "Can you go up and get Aunt Myrtle?" He said, "Yes, Mommy."

I said, "Take a flashlight, and don't be afraid of the snake. You will have to walk right by it, but remember it's dead."

He said, "I will be brave, Mommy. I won't be afraid."

We said a prayer to ask God to take care of Dallas. Then, he turned to little Katy standing behind him quietly watching and listening, and said, "Now, Katy, you take good care of Mommy while I'm gone." Katy wasn't talking yet, but she seemed to understand.

After Dallas left, Katy resumed the cold cloth on the forehead duty. However, being positioned behind Dallas through all of his care, all she saw was him bend over, do something with his hands, and stand back up. So she faithfully copied the movements she had seen. She bent over me, held my nose for a few seconds, then released it and stood up straight again. Then she bent over, held my nose, released it, and stood up, "taking care" of Mommy like her big brother told her to do.

This went on for the next forty-five minutes until Dallas returned with Aunt Myrtle. Katy's "helpfulness" kept my mind off the pain in my toe. Every time she stood back up, I would smile and thank her for helping Mommy.

When Dallas returned with Aunt Myrtle, we prayed that my toe could be fixed without surgery. Aunt Myrtle drove us to the emergency room where a doctor pulled my toe out and back up into place, without surgery. *Ouch*! He taped it to the other toe until the break could heal.

God protected my little boy walking up a country road by himself in the dark, He helped my baby girl to keep me distracted from the pain, and He fixed my toe, *so it has never hurt since.* God is so Good!

"He healeth the broken in heart, and bindeth up their wounds" (Ps. 147:3).

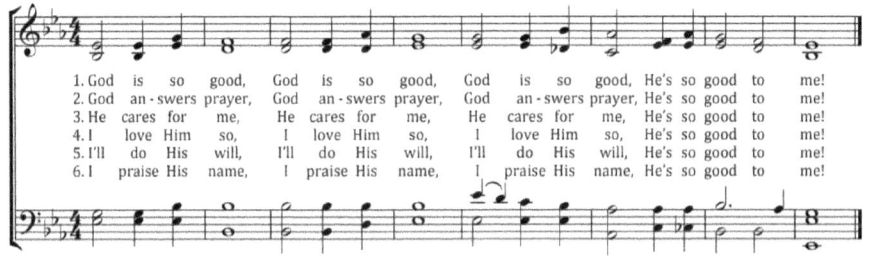

God Is So Good

O give thanks unto the Lord; for he is good; for his mercy endureth for ever. 1 Chr. 16:34

1. God is so good, God is so good, God is so good, He's so good to me!
2. God answers prayer, God answers prayer, God answers prayer, He's so good to me!
3. He cares for me, He cares for me, He cares for me, He's so good to me!
4. I love Him so, I love Him so, I love Him so, He's so good to me!
5. I'll do His will, I'll do His will, I'll do His will, He's so good to me!
6. I praise His name, I praise His name, I praise His name, He's so good to me!

WORDS: *attr. to* Velna A. Ledin, 1933; v.2-6 author unknown. MUSIC: V. A. L., 1933. Public Domain.

Mouth of Babes

When my children were young, we decided to have a big yard sale and clean out our house to make room for our growing family. As we were sorting through things, we came across items that had belonged to my mother when she was living. As I slowly sorted through them, remembering her and the meaning of each of these items, I broke down crying. Each item brought more and more memories—beautiful memories—and now sad memories, because she was no longer with us.

I sat in a chair holding Mother's things, sobbing uncontrollably, while other family members worked around me, unpacking and arranging for the yard sale. No one said anything to me until my nine-year-old son, Dallas, came up to me and sweetly said, "Mommy, if Jesus comes tomorrow, are you going to sit here and hold Grandma's stuff, or are you going with Jesus to heaven and see Grandma herself?"

WOW! What a thought! All of a sudden, those material things didn't seem so "all-fired" important anymore. And, no, they did not mean more to me than going to heaven. Dallas was right! Thinking of his words made it so much easier to get rid of the things we did not need anymore.

"And take heed to yourselves, lest at any time ... cares of this life ... come upon you unawares. For as a snare shall it come on all them that dwell on the face of the whole earth" (Luke 21:34, 35).

Physical Meltdown

Once, when my husband got laid off from his job, I got two jobs to try to keep up our income. I worked nights 11–7 in a nursing home, taking total care of twenty-six patients all night with no breaks. I also had another job taking care of a lady in the daytime in her home. My husband was with the children at night, but gone all day looking for another job. The children were ages eight and three.

God worked it out so that in my day job I could take my three-year-old daughter with me, and even my eight-year old could come there after he got out of school every day. That worked out great … or so I thought.

After I got off work in the mornings, and took my son to school, I would try to sleep for an hour or two before going to my day job. I would put some toys on the floor in the living room beside the couch for my precious little girl to play with beside me, so she wouldn't think she was all alone and be afraid. Then I would explain, "Mommy's going to sleep for an hour, and you can play right here beside me."

"Okay, Mommy," was her sweet reply.

But, of course, a three-year-old has no clue how long an hour is. So, in five minutes, a sweet thumb and finger would gently take hold of my nose and wiggle it slightly (the nose must have looked to her like my handle) as her sweet little voice said, "Mommy, has it been an hour?"

"No, honey, keep playing."

"Okay, Mommy."

After a few more minutes, maybe ten at the most, another nose wiggle, then, "Mommy, has it been an hour?" Thus went my nap time!

One afternoon while both of my children were with me at the lady's house, I had just walked into her kitchen, when the room started going around horizontally. The next minute it also started going vertically, so I couldn't see. Not wanting to fall and not being able to tell which way was down, I called my son to come take my hand and help me down gently to the floor as I fainted.

Still not being able to see when we got to the doctor's office, I could hear the doctor talking to my cousin, Bernice, whom Dallas had called to come to the lady's house to get us and take me to the doctor. He was saying, "She has a 50/50 chance of making it. Her body's vital force is worn out from not enough sleep. She's almost used it up. She has to have complete bed rest."

So I lay on the couch at home for three weeks with what turned out to be a severe inner ear infection. Every time I opened my eyes and tried to move, I fell off the couch, because I still couldn't tell which way was up. At the end of three weeks, I was starting to walk a few steps and was getting well, we thought, when suddenly all three of us were exposed to chicken pox! We each one got them. Katy got a few spots but Dallas was covered with the pox, so he was pretty miserable. As an adult, with my immune system totally rundown, I had a bad case, which lasted for two months. After two months, the pox went into encephalitis, and later, while I still had that, I got scarlet fever.

The doctors were really worried that I was too worn down to get well, as I kept getting worse. They said nothing could be done and being in the hospital wouldn't help either. What I needed was total bed rest and sleep.

But God was with me. He was teaching me to slow down and take better care of my body; to take time for Him; to "take time to smell the roses" as the saying goes.

"The LORD will strengthen him upon the bed of languishing: thou wilt make all his bed in his sickness" (Ps. 41:3).

I lay at home for eleven months on total bed rest. God guided my (by then) nine-year-old son and fouryear-old daughter, who took wonderful care of me. Their dad had found a job by now, and so was gone fourteen hours during the day. Precious church people and other friends baked food and brought it to our house. They would give it to Dallas at the door with instructions how to heat it up. No one wanted to come inside our house for fear of catching my illness.

On school days, Dallas left the house early every morning to be on time, walking one-and-a-half miles to school, but sometimes was able to catch a ride. In the afternoon, he walked home. When Dallas was home, he cleaned house, cooked meals for the three of us, and made sure his sister ate. Sometimes I would wake up and it was already after lunch time. I would call Dallas into my room and say, "Honey, it's past time to eat; do you have something to fix?"

He would always answer with, "We already ate, Mommy. We had a green vegetable, a yellow vegetable, an entree that someone brought, and a salad." Then he would bring a plate of food to me. God helped him to be very faithful to fix well-balanced meals, that he had been learning about while helping me in the kitchen prior to my illness.

Dallas mowed our lawn when it was needed. Katy helped him by picking up sticks. Then, as winter started coming on, he split the wood for the wood stove. At age nine, that got his muscles growing bigger. One day when I woke up, I heard Dallas very sternly talking to his little four-year-old sister. He was saying "Katy Annette Roberts, I just cleaned your room yesterday! Why is it messed up again today? What happened to it?" So he was even helping his little sister clean her room!

God can make a blessing out of anything! My children were such a blessing to me while I was so sick for so long. Lying there day after day, God used many things and people—including my children—to keep me encouraged. One particular quote was a huge blessing to me. My dear friend and children's teacher, Margaret, wrote it out for me and decorated it with colorful artwork and flowers on a card to sit on my bedside table for me to read every day. It said, "Often your mind may be clouded because of pain. Then do not try to think. You know that Jesus loves you. He understands your weakness. You may do His will by simply resting in His arms" (White, *The Ministry of Healing*, 251). That was so encouraging that I memorized it!

My children would take me out to sit in the sun on the porch. God made the sun to heal and give a person strength. It helped me so much!

After eleven months, I was able to sit up for longer periods of time, and soon I was up helping my children with all the duties they had been doing. God was teaching me in all this sickness to slow down and be contented and at peace.

He says, "Be still, and know that I am God" (Ps. 46:10).

Sharing

When my daughter Katy was just four years old, she only had two dresses to her name. She saved them for church. So, one Sabbath she would wear one, the next Sabbath she would wear the other one, back and forth.

One Sunday, a family came to our home to visit. They had three boys and one little girl Katy's age. Katy and Sarah had a good time playing together in Katy's room, while the boys played outside with the dog. Sarah mentioned to Katy that she didn't have any church clothes to wear and no dresses at all. Katy had been learning the "Sharing Song" in Sabbath School, where they practiced sharing their dollies and toys. She took that advice seriously and went a step further.

Katy and Sarah quietly came into where the adults were visiting, and Katy came up to me and whispered in my ear, "Mommy, can I give Sarah one of my dresses? I have two."

I excused myself from the others and went with Katy to her bedroom closet. One of her two dresses was just beautiful on her—the other one was just kind of ordinary. Katy said, "Mommy, can I give her my prettiest one?"

My first thought was selfish. I thought, "No way! We'll give her the one that is not so pretty." But watching Katy's excitement at wanting to share her most beautiful dress, I forced a smile and said, "Yes, honey, you can give her the pretty one."

Katy was ecstatic, and took the dress to Sarah, who now was sitting in the living room with her parents. Sarah's parents were so surprised and super happy! Her mother said, "She hasn't had any dresses."

After the family left, the thought hit me, "Now, Katy will have to wear the same dress every Sabbath." There's nothing wrong with that, but we always want the best for our children. However, we must remember that if we give the best of what we have, then God will take care of us.

But this was not a surprise to our *awesome* God! He already had made provision for His little four-year-old warrior of faith. On Tuesday, even before the next Sabbath, a family with three girls brought to us a big box full of forty dresses! The smallest were Katy's size at the time, the next were one size up, and the largest were three sizes up, so she could grow into them.

God keeps His promises and rewarded Katy's unselfish Christian attitude with more blessings from God than she had room to receive.

"... Prove me now herewith, saith the LORD of hosts, if I will not open you the windows of heaven, and pour you out a blessing, that there shall not be room enough to receive it" (Mal. 3:10).

Now Katy had more beautiful dresses than we could even get into her closet! And enough dresses to last for years to come.

Oh, for the unselfish faith of a child!

"... Verily I say unto you, Except ye be converted, and become as little children, ye shall not enter into the kingdom of heaven. Whosoever therefore shall humble himself as this little child, the same is greatest in the kingdom of heaven" (Matt. 18:3, 4).

The Waitress

God impressed me many years ago to always leave a little tract with my tip for the server when eating out. These small tracts are about various Bible subjects, but all tell that Jesus loves us, and died for each one of us, to deliver us from sin and Satan and his many temptations.

My family and I "happened" to eat at a restaurant where we had just eaten the week before. We rarely ate out—much less two weeks in a row—and to go to the same place was unheard of. However, with God there are no "accidents," and this second time we entered and stood at the waiting area to be seated. As we looked around, I noticed a waitress across the dining room look up from the table that she was waiting on and see us. She came rushing around the tables right up to us. She seated us at a table, and said, "I just wanted to thank you for that little pamphlet you left at my table last week. I had decided that I had no reason to keep on living, and had planned to end it all that night when I got back home. My mother had just died, and my husband had left me, and my car had broken down." She named a couple other discouraging things that had happened to her recently.

She was now the epitome of happiness, smiling at everyone. Knowing Jesus loved her was everything to her

Continuing, she said, "I thought no one loved me, and I just couldn't take any more. When I got off at 11:00 that night and went home, I was standing beside my kitchen table, unloading my uniform pockets. I was taking out my tips, when there was the pamphlet that you gave me. I decided to read it first before I took the pills." Then, with a big smile, she said, "And, look! Here I am! I know now that Jesus loves me!"

She squeezed my hand and was off to another table. She was now the epitome of happiness, smiling at everyone. Knowing Jesus loved her was everything to her.

"And I, if I be lifted up from the earth, will draw all men unto me" (John 12:32).

Strawberry Vines

"God, PLEASE help me with this problem."

I pray this every day. In fact, I pray it several times a day. Isn't that what I am supposed to do? Ask God to help me with my problems? Then why doesn't He help? Why am I still struggling with the same problems?

Over and over these questions go through my head. All the time it seems that God is not doing anything for my problems. Then my blood pressure goes up, followed by a trip to the doctor, then a new medicine that doesn't work any better than the last one. It's a vicious cycle.

One day, after more tests, the doctor made a new discovery. "Negative thoughts make your blood pressure go up," he said to me.

"Huh?"

"Yes, you have malignant hypertension."

"Oh my! That sounds scary. You mean I have cancer?"

"No. But it means that anything can make your blood pressure go up, especially anything negative. From now on, you HAVE to keep your mind on positive thoughts."

"Wow!" I thought as I drove home. "How can I keep my mind on positive thoughts in a negative world?" Of course, at that very moment, the latest financial problem in my life came to mind.

Oh dear! "Okay, God, now You have to help me with this problem, because it's very negative and now I am not supposed to think negatively, because my blood pressure will go up. HELP!!!"

Right then, very sweetly and patiently, God brought to my mind John 14:1–3, which says, *"Let not your heart be troubled:* ye believe in God, believe also in me. In My Father's house are many mansions: if it were not so, I would have told you. I go to prepare a place for you. And if I go and prepare a place for you, I will come again, and receive you unto myself; that where I am, there ye may be also" (emphasis added).

The thought to not let my heart be troubled was very encouraging, and that God is preparing mansions for us in heaven was exciting to me! Then, after He re-creates this earth, we will have our homes in the new earth, as it is written in Isaiah 65:21, 22: "And they shall build houses, and inhabit them; and they shall plant vineyards, and eat the fruit of them. They shall not build, and another inhabit; they shall not plant, and another eat: for as the days of a tree are the days of my people, and mine elect shall long enjoy the work of their hands." Revelation 21:1 also tells us about this new earth.: "And I saw a new heaven and a new earth: for the first heaven and the first earth were passed away; and there was no more sea."

Since I enjoy home decorating, I immediately started designing my home in the new earth. My mind raced! WOW!! How exciting!!! Low and behold, as I enthusiastically planned my home, my blood pressure started coming down!

As I looked around at my simple house here, I thought, "In the new earth, what if we didn't have walls like these, with drywall, paint, paneling, etc.? What if we had floor-to-ceiling ... um, say, *strawberry vines?* Then you could sit back in your 'easy chair' and pick a strawberry from your 'wall.' In another room, there could be floor-to-ceiling orange blossoms, another room, floor-to ceiling gardenias, and across the top, for the ceiling, gorgeous purple wisteria hanging down. Think of the beautiful fragrance of each room. No more artificial room deodorizers. It's all natural and real."

After some time of this inspired planning, I realized my blood pressure had come down and was normal, leaving no more headaches or tension of any sort. That's when God showed me that I should find a positive thought, and when I have a problem, I should turn it totally over to Him and let Him handle it, and then I should think of my positive thought.

This is the way it works: First, I get my positive thought that God gave to me, which for me is my strawberry vines planning. Next, I get on my knees and tell God all about my problem. In this case, it was finances. I had to tell God every single thing about the problem … tell Him what is happening, tell Him how I feel, tell Him about the other person (if someone else is involved), and every tidbit about this one problem. He, of course, already knows everything about it, though. I am not telling Him for His sake, but for mine, because I don't want to have a time later that I think, "oh, did I tell God this part?" So, now, while I'm on my knees, I tell Him the whole "kit and kaboodle" of it. In my prayer to God, I include, "If there's something You want me to do, tell me so I'll know it's from You without a doubt. Otherwise, You handle it and I won't think of it anymore."

When I'm finished telling Him, I get up off my knees, and immediately, Satan hits me with the problem. Now, it's no longer MY problem. I just turned it over to God, so I don't have to think about it any longer. So now, when Satan hits, I look up and say, "God, here it is—You take it," and force my mind to think of my strawberry vines. There is a saying that reminds us, "Prayer is where burdens change shoulders." Now, I know that for myself.

They say it takes about three weeks to change a habit, so for the first three or four weeks it's really a constant battle. Like the song says, we have to take it "moment by moment." Satan tries, and tries again, to bring me down, but after my mind gets in the habit of thinking my positive thought, I say, "God, here it is—You take it," and my mind automatically goes to happier things.

I have also learned that it is better for me to deal with one problem at a time. While on my knees telling God all about the ONE problem, I don't want to get sidetracked thinking of another problem, and leave something out and worry or think of it later. The idea is NOT to allow yourself to dwell on the problem ever again once you have given it to Jesus. You can do this with each problem that comes up, until you have given ALL of them to God.

That, I learned, is totally turning my problem over to God. Always before, I would say, "God, please take care of my problem;" then I would continue to try to figure it out and worry and worry and fret and fret, and no solutions would transpire. But once I learned to *totally* give the problem to God and not think about it anymore except to pray, the problems got solved, taken care of in all kinds of ways.

As it says in the book, *Desire of Ages*, "Our heavenly Father has a thousand ways to provide for us, of which we know nothing" (White, 330).

While our simple minds can only think of one or two ways to deal with something (and even then they will likely be inferior), God's omnipotent creativity and love for us can be trusted to take care of us always.

One day, as I was telling a friend about my strawberry vines, she said, "Well, I like waterfalls." So I said, "Okay, *your* positive thought can be waterfalls."

A month later, the same friend called crying. I said, "What about your waterfalls?"

Tearfully, she answered, "I WAS thinking of my waterfalls, but a man was walking across the top and he fell!"

That's when I realized that our positive thought has to be about Jesus or heaven, so there won't ever be any negative connotation to it. It's so exciting, totally turning everything over to God and watching Him take care of it!

Of course, Satan wants to spoil this, too. He hates positive, Christ-centered thoughts. So one day, as I started telling my "strawberry vines" discovery to a new lady, she interrupted by saying, "There's no such thing as strawberry vines." For a moment, my whole countenance fell through the floor—I felt so discouraged.

> *It's so exciting, totally turning everything over to God and watching Him take care of it*

But God intervened, and a big smile came over my face, and out of my mouth came, "Well, there could be strawberry vines in heaven."

The lady said, "Oh yes, I guess so," and then she, too, was smiling and happy again. A few short years after God showed me the strawberry vines, an evangelist came to our church for a series of meetings. The last night of the meetings, he spoke on heaven. Toward the end of the meeting, he asked, "Have any of you ever planned your home in the new earth?"

Sitting in the middle of the full auditorium, I was so excited I almost jumped up out of my seat and almost yelled, "Yes, I have." Thankfully, I didn't squeal out.

The speaker said, "In the new earth, I'm going to have one wall in my house made of crushed diamonds, so it can reflect the beautiful light from God."

WOW! I never thought of jewels. I had designed my whole house with vegetation. But, now that I know about the jewels, I'm excitedly redesigning my home in the new earth and have a whole new "positive thought."

God impressed a fellow church member, Jeremy, once to use the following illustration in a sermon. Holding up his left hand, he said, "This represents my problem. This is the way we ask God to help us with our problem." Looking at his left hand, he said, "God, help me with my problem, help me with my problem, help me with my problem," as he slowly lowered the left hand all the way to the floor, constantly staring at it.

Then he stood up and said, "This is the way we *should* ask God to help us." He held up his right hand to represent his problem. "God, help me with my problem, please help me with my problem," as he stared at his right hand raising it upward and looking toward heaven. He said, "we look at and dwell on our problem instead of looking to and dwelling on Jesus as the solution for our problem."

Another way to keep our lives positive—and it always brings my blood pressure down—is to study the gospels of Matthew, Mark, Luke, and John in the Bible. I have also discovered that reading the book on Christ's life called *The Desire of Ages* by E.G. White brings my blood pressure back to normal.

It must be because reading either of these keeps my mind on Jesus, contemplating His life, dwelling on Him instead of me and my problems.

Yes, God DOES do something about my problems. He DOES listen. The only reason I still struggle with the same problem, If I do, is because of me. I haven't *totally* turned the problem over to Him. Now, with God's idea of my "strawberry vines" I am learning to turn everything, one at a time, over to Him.

God now takes care of my problems. He works with me, teaching me daily to trust totally in Him. And this same God in heaven will take care of your problems, too! He LOVES working together with you. So let Him!!!!

"*Come unto me, all ye that labour and are heavy laden, and I will give you rest*" (Matt. 11:28).

The Bath Bee

One night, I was taking a shower and washing my hair. I had my eyes closed and my head back under the water, rinsing. Suddenly, I felt what I thought was a bee sting my foot. WOW! It had to be a really big bee to hurt that bad!

I turned the water off to look for that super big bee, all the time thinking, "To start with, it's nighttime, and bees aren't out at night. Plus, I am inside, not outside, and how can a bee survive in the shower with all this water?" No matter where I looked, I could not find that bee. Finally, I dried off, put my gown on, and went to bed.

The next morning, I was in the kitchen fixing breakfast. The kids came in saying, "There is no hot water for our showers." I checked the kitchen faucet. Sure enough—no hot water. So, I called my "fix anything" daddy, who lived half-an-hour away. He came over, and said, "Let's check the water heater." At that time, the water heater was in the basement, directly under the bathroom. Daddy and I went down there. To our horror, the water heater had caught on fire and was partially burnt up. The part that was left was all melted down and black!

My electrician daddy said, "Wow! It's a good thing no one was in the shower! This would have electrocuted and killed them!"

I told him about the bee sting, and he said, "That wasn't a bee sting; that was the electric charge from the burning water heater!" Daddy and I looked at each other, wondering what kept the water heater from catching the house on fire and burning it down.

Daddy said, "It had to be an angel that put out this fire, saving your life from the electrical charge, and the whole house from burning to the ground last night."

Dear reader, when we all get to heaven, we will be able to ask our angel about all the many times they saved our lives and we didn't even know about it.

WOW! How exciting!

"There shall no evil befall thee, neither shall any plague come nigh thy dwelling. For He shall give his angels charge over thee, to keep thee in all thy ways" (Ps. 91:10, 11).

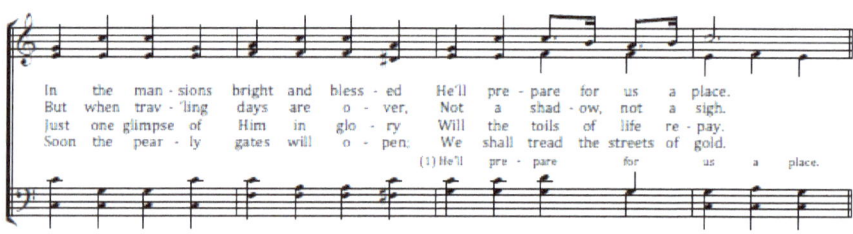
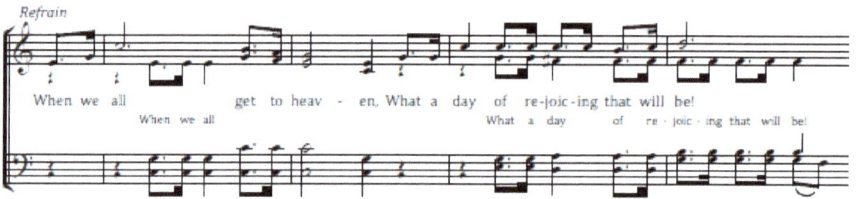
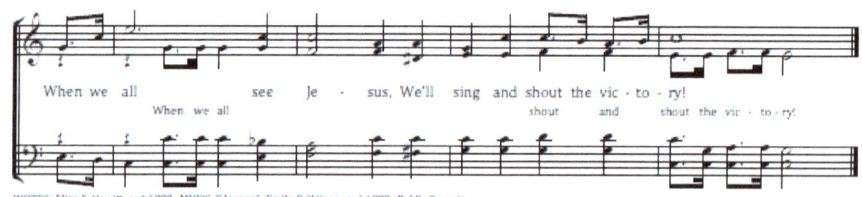

God's Leading

To be honest with you, I really don't know exactly where this story started. Every time I think of a start and get it written down, then I think of something that happened even before that to lead up to it. So, I will just start!!!

After high school, my son, Dallas, had full intentions of becoming a forest ranger. He has always loved the outdoors, and God helped him learn many things in the various lines of nature. He can identify, and has worked with, many kinds of birds, rocks, fungi, flowers, trees, etc. He had already completed one course in wildlife and forestry conservation and received his diploma.

Then, one day in late spring of 1993, Dallas came to me and said, "I've been praying about it, and I feel that I want to help save lives." So, he applied to a local college to take the paramedic course that fall. All went well until about two weeks before his classes were to begin. His adviser called from the college and said, "I'm sorry, but this class is full; you won't be able to attend this year." She couldn't figure out the reason for the short notice, either.

Dallas continued with his own business, doing different jobs for people—painting, construction, yard work, or whatever they needed done. Yet he continued to pray that God would use him in some way. This was a prayer that I, too, was praying, but I didn't know that he was.

Dallas had talked about mission service several times, but I didn't think there was a chance of that, since he had not gone to a college that sends out student missionaries. After three months of not knowing what to do, I prayed, "God, do something! Please don't let Dallas lose his desire to work for you." Two days after I prayed that prayer, a phone call came—the one that started everything.

I've always known that God closes the doors that we should not enter, and opens the doors that take us down His path, but I had no idea He'd even take them off of their hinges!!!

The phone call came the weekend before Thanksgiving. A friend of ours in Virginia called and told us of an advertisement wanting people to teach Bible and English in Russia. Dallas was gone that weekend and didn't get home until late Monday night, so he did not learn of the opportunity until Tuesday morning.

We all prayed about it and by Tuesday night, Dallas had made his decision. He wanted to answer the call to Russia. This would definitely be a way to "help save lives" for eternity.

The next morning, Wednesday, I called Silver Spring, Maryland. The assistant director for the organization sending teachers to Russia said that she would send Dallas some forms to fill out, but meantime to try to work on his passport, because, if at all possible, they needed him to board the plane on December 27, only four-and-a-half weeks away!!

I called the passport office and simply asked, "What do I do to get a passport for my son to go to Russia to teach?"

The man in the passport office said, "You'll need money, driver's license, and a certified birth certificate." Then he added, "Call your congressman's office and they can help you get it sooner. Otherwise, it will take six to eight weeks." I had not mentioned our short time deadline.

The lady in the congressman's office said, "Why did he (meaning the passport man) tell you that so soon? He never tells people to call us until they've tried everything else first." God already had the ball rolling.

I called the vital records office of the state of Tennessee, where Dallas was born, to get the certified birth certificate. The lady that I reached was not the least bit interested in helping me. Finally she said, "Well, okay, I can start the processing, but it will take two weeks." Very distraughtly, I told her to go ahead and get started on it. That was late Wednesday afternoon. The next day was Thanksgiving. All the offices were also closed on Friday, so that left us no alternative but to wait until Monday.

We prayed about it all weekend, and Monday morning I had the strongest urge to call back to the vital records office, and this time I got a different lady. I told her the same story about how much time we had, and she said, "I'll get right on it." The certified birth certificate was here in our hands the next morning at 11:00! We rushed to the passport office and then to the congressman's office. They were all so very helpful, and got everything on its way to Washington, DC, for his passport. The passport came in one week and one day! That was a miracle in itself.

Also on that Tuesday morning, it occurred to me that Dallas would need medical checkups before he went away for a whole year to another country. So, I called the office of our dentist, Dr. Bill Moore, fully expecting them to say they would try to work him in sometime in the next two or three weeks, because they are always full. The receptionist said, "We have an opening this afternoon at 2:30." I couldn't help but squeal right on the phone, because then I thought that would allow a couple of weeks to work Dallas in again if he needed more work done.

When Dallas came out of his 2:30 appointment, he said he needed more work, but Dr. Moore had already made an appointment for him the next morning at 8:00. All of that was taken care of in less than twenty-four hours.

God works fast!!

Dallas had just had an eye exam the month before, so I called to order a year's supply of contacts for him. About half-an-hour after we hung up, the ophthalmic assistant called back and asked, "What about his solution for his contacts?" There are several different ones and we needed his specific brand.

I said, "Oh, dear, I forgot all about that." Knowing that would be yet a lot more expense, I said, "How much is it?"

She said, "It just went on sale, today! We've never had a sale like this before; I don't even know why we're having this sale." (But you and I do … God is still opening doors).

The next day, our family doctor, Dr. Randy Tryon, called and said he had heard about Dallas going to Russia and would like to help. An appointment was made. Not only did Dr. Tryon give Dallas a free physical, but also part of his immunization shots, a special water filter, so Dallas could filter and drink the water over there, and a whole pharmacy of medicines to take to Russia with him, in case he needed them for himself or for other people.

There was one shot still needed that we could not locate. Finally, after praying, we found it (the last week) in another county. When we got to that clinic, a lady took us right back to the immunization office. To our surprise, she was a Seventh-day Adventist and had served five years as a missionary in Africa. Because of this, she was full of information and travel tips. Also, she showed us a film on overseas traveling, how to adjust to time change, jet lag, and to the food and water. Then, to top it off, she had personal friends already in Moscow who she knew would be willing to help in any way they could.

You see what I mean about God swinging the doors wide open, even off their hinges? But that's not all. It seemed like God walked through every door before us, preparing the way even in our purchases. Dallas didn't have many clothes, and especially really warm ones. Looking at

Moscow on the map, it appears to be at the same latitude as Canada. So we presumed that it is quite cold.

And it was currently winter!! BRRR! So away we went to buy a few warm clothes. Every single thing we had to buy not only was on sale, but was at least 40% off its regular price! One item, a heavy winter coat, normally very expensive, was 75% off its regular price. And this was the beginning of winter, not the sale at the end of winter. Then, when the clerk heard the story of Russia, she knocked off another 16%!

> *You see what I mean about God swinging the doors wide open, even off their hinges? But that's not all. It seemed like God walked through every door before us, preparing the way*

Isn't God *awesome!?* He loves us and cares about every aspect of our lives. Like I said before, not only did God open the doors wide for Dallas to go and work for Him—but He led the way through the doors!

Dallas left from National Airport in Washington, DC, on December 27, 1993, right on time!

Like I said before, I can't seem to find the beginning of this story. Nine months before Dallas left, God helped his dad to find a job and stay at home with Dallas (and all of us). His dad had been driving a truck for years and now got to be home with his son before Dallas left for a year.

"Thus saith the LORD, thy Redeemer, the Holy One of Israel; I am the LORD thy God which teacheth thee to profit, which leadeth thee by the way that thou shouldest go" (Isa. 48:17).

The "Mean" Girl

I rode the Greyhound bus out west to see my daughter, Katy, when she was in college in South Dakota. The trip took fifty hours. I had taken a paper grocery bag full of magazines, pamphlets, and books on as many good subjects as I could get my hands on. I set the bag on the floor at my feet, so, as I met the various travelers, talked to them, and learned of their concerns, I could hopefully give them some helpful information.

After hours of traveling and visiting, most everyone on this particular bus had a piece of the literature from the bag—except the girl that sat on the back seat of the bus next to the bathroom. She was the meanest looking girl I had ever seen. She dressed like a man and walked like a man. She carried her shoulders up and slightly forward when walking. Her arms hung out and down, and her fingers stayed partially curled like a body builder. On her face was a horrible scowl, like "you look at me and I will HIT you." Truthfully, I was afraid of her.

When the bus stopped to let the smokers off to smoke, she always got off and "hung out" with the men. (The men grouped together in one area and the women grouped together over in another.) Then, when they would all get back on the bus, I would catch myself leaning the other way as this girl walked past my seat, so as to be out of the way if she decided to hit someone.

As the bus started rolling again, the Holy Spirit started working on me. "Most everyone has some literature except that girl! Most everyone has some literature except THAT GIRL."

"I know, Lord," I said in my mind, "but please don't make me give HER something; she will hit me, or worse."

"THAT GIRL!"

"No, Lord, no, please no."

"THAT GIRL!!"

This battle went on within me until my eyes were watering. I knew God was right, but I was SO scared. I could just picture giving her something and her going into a rage, throwing the book at me, the bus stopping, and a big fight breaking out.

Finally, in dire frustration with myself, I said, "Okay God, I'll give her something, but please don't let it be *Steps to Christ*." I just knew that if she saw the word Christ (or any holy word) on it she would for sure yell or throw it at me. Then I thought, "Oh, horrors," and added, "please, definitely don't let it be the *Steps to Christ* with the picture of Jesus on the front." I knew that would do me in for sure.

There were other books that I *could* give her, like one called *Happiness Digest*, which is the same book with a different cover. So I stuck my hand down in the literature bag, not even knowing what was left in there, and told God, "You put into my hand what you want me to give her."

And, don't you know, I pulled my hand up out of the bag, and there was God's choice in my hand, *Steps to Christ*, **with** the picture of Jesus on the front! But I didn't even have time to argue. "Something" took a hold of my arm, lifted me up out of my seat, turned me around, and there I was walking to the back of the bus toward the "mean girl." I was so scared; I was shaking like a leaf. When I got to her seat, I stiffened up, held out the book, shaking, and in a weak, shaky voice, I said, "I … uh … brought some … uh … extra … uh … reading material, and thought … uh… I would share some … uh … with you."

The girl glared at me and her mouth dropped wide open. Then she glared at the book and then back at me. She reached out and took the book, saying in slow words, "Thanks … I needed this."

Then MY mouth dropped wide open to the floor. "You're welcome," I pushed out as I fled back to my seat, still shaking profusely. I sat there, praying for her as God calmed me down.

The first time the bus stopped after that, as the girl was getting off to smoke, she stopped next to my seat. Her finger was in the book; she had already read the first two chapters. She said, "I want to tell you something. I just left Connecticut, where my mother lives, and I'm on my way to San Francisco, where I live. We just buried my twenty-three-year-old brother in Connecticut, and six weeks ago we buried my stepfather. My mother is so depressed she doesn't want to live anymore. She wants to kill herself. I will have finished this book by the time I get home and I will send it to her. It will save her life."

Whoever God puts in front of us is who He wants us to help or witness to. God knew exactly what that girl needed. I didn't know

That's when I learned to *not* pick and choose WHO to witness to. It's not up to me. Whoever God puts in front of us is who He wants us to help or witness to. God knew exactly what that girl needed. I didn't know. This also taught me that I should not judge people by what I THINK they look like. This girl was desperate and hurting inside, not "mean" at all!

We are on this earth to help others find a better life, and to do God's will, not our own. When Jesus was on this earth, He never made plans for Himself. Every day, He did the will of His Father. (See *Desire of Ages*, by E.G. White, page 208.2 and John 6:38.)

Shouldn't we, too?

Big Miracles, Few Words

When I was ten years old, my parents and I lived in Florida. Because Daddy couldn't leave his job then, Mother was in charge of having our cottage built in the mountains of North Carolina one summer.

At the end of the summer, when Mother and I were leaving our newly-built mountain home to go back to Florida, Mother prayed, "God, please protect my country home and don't allow any kind of bugs to infest, or anyone to break in."

Mother's "mountain home" sat there for over fourteen years, completely furnished, including books, clothing, fully-equipped kitchen, the whole works, and never one bug was in it … no moths, mice, silverfish, no varmints at all, not even spider webs!

Except for a small amount of dust, the house was exactly the same each summer as we had left it the year before. Even the years after she died and no one lived in the house at all for years at a time, it was totally free of critters. God answered Mother's prayer for her mountain home.

It wasn't just inside that God protected Mother's home. Even the outside security light that had twenty-seven bullet holes in it from someone trying to shoot it out was still burning!

"Because thou hast made the Lord, which is my refuge, even the most High, thy habitation; There shall no evil befall thee, neither shall any plague come nigh thy dwelling" (Ps. 91:9, 10).

* * *

Many years later, after my children's Daddy left us, the first thing that happened was that God impressed my cousins—my Uncle Paul's family (parents, children, and grandchildren)—to collect money among themselves, actually almost a thousand dollars, and God impressed cousin Victor to bring it all to me. What a wonderful surprise! God doesn't do things halfway! This helped to pay my bills for quite a while, until other money started coming in and other sources of income began to come together. God used my precious cousins first, and then many other people, to get us through this crisis. That was so special of them to let God use them in this way!

"And they that know thy name will put their trust in thee: for thou, Lord, hast not forsaken them that seek thee" (Ps. 9:10).

* * *

Another miracle, after my husband left, was when a financial advisor from my church came to me and volunteered his financial services to help work out a budget with my newly meager income.

I was so appreciative of his time and effort in helping me. We set a time, and he came to our home. After we talked a bit, he sat down at the table and started working, using receipts, bills, statements, and all of my financial records.

After two whole hours of silent, intensive study and figuring, he laid down his pen, turned off his calculator, and, looking up at me as I walked into the room, he said, "Rita, you are paying out $240 more on bills a month than you are bringing in! That is humanly impossible! God is DEFINITELY taking care of you!"

Even in this case, other people could see **GOD IN MY LIFE!**

"For he shall deliver the needy when he crieth; the poor also, and him that hath no helper" (Ps. 72:12).

My Friend Mildred

Mildred was older than me. She was a beautiful woman inside and out! I never saw her without a happy smile on her face. She lived up the street and around the corner from our home in Madison, Tennessee. We always had a good time laughing and talking together.

I knew her sons were grown and lived in different states, but I didn't know anything about her husband since she was living alone. So, one day I asked about her husband, and this is the story she told me.

She and her husband Roy and their two little boys, aged about two and five at the time, lived on the fourteenth floor of an apartment building in New York City. They were so very happy. Roy worked all day while Mildred was home taking care of the boys, cooking, and keeping house for all of them. For her, life was perfect.

One day, while Mildred and the boys were home, she received a horrible phone call. There had been a bad accident at work and Roy had been killed. Totally shocked and devastated, Mildred had no idea what to do.

Well-meaning friends tried to "comfort" her with their belief that God needed her husband, so He took him, and Roy was now in heaven looking down on her, watching her. "He's happy and fine there with God, so don't worry about him," they kept telling her.

To devastated Mildred, these words and the very idea of this thought was NOT comforting. Through her tears and distress, she started hating God. She yelled at those people when they "comforted" her that way.

"God doesn't need him more than I do! Who's going to support our two little boys? Who will help me with them? Who will support us and buy our food and pay our rent? Who will take care of us? God is *mean* to take Roy. I need him myself. Our boys need their daddy."

Still screaming, she yelled, "I hate God! I hate God! I hate God! He had no business taking our daddy. I NEED him—God doesn't!" as she broke into sobs again.

Day after day, Mildred hated God more and more! She even found herself hating Roy, her dearly beloved husband, now that he was up there happy and content with no worries—looking down on her struggling so.

Mildred realized she now had to find a job—but she had never received any higher education of any kind, so what could she do? She had no money to pay a babysitter for her little boys, either.

Finally, the only job Mildred could find was cleaning toilets in office buildings all night. So, every night Mildred got her little boys to bed, waited till they were asleep, then would lock the door tight and leave them home all alone for the night. This broke her heart every time she had to quietly shut that door.

She said her hands would be bleeding from all the scrubbing by the time she was walking home the next morning. She would unlock the door and go in to her darling little boys—hopefully still sleeping.

Weeks and months passed. By now, with her painful calloused hands, and so very tired from working every night, Mildred totally hated God, and even hated Roy. She thought that God had selfishly taken her husband with no thought of her and the little boys. She said, "I HATED GOD!"

Still screaming, she yelled, "I hate God! I hate God! I hate God! He had no business taking our daddy. I NEED him—God doesn't!" as she broke into sobs again

Then, Mildred told me that one Saturday morning, as she was walking to her apartment from work, "I heard some pretty music. It was the most beautiful music I had *ever* heard."

She started following the music sound, up one street and down another, until she came to a church. Mildred definitely did NOT want anything to do with the mean God—but she DID want to hear the rest of that pretty music.

So she decided she would go up the steps to the church, go inside, and sit on the back row where no one would see her. Then, when the music was over, she would hurry out the door and no one would know, and she wouldn't have to hear any of that "stuff" about God.

Mildred slipped inside and sat on the back pew closest to the door. As she sat down behind a man and woman, the woman turned around, extended her hand and whispered, "So glad you're here."

Mildred smiled and shook her hand. The woman turned partly back toward the front, but kept holding onto Mildred's hand. When the music was over, Mildred tried to pull her hand loose from the other woman to get up to leave—but she couldn't pull her hand out of the lady's hand.

Then the prayer was said. As soon as the minister said "amen," he left the pulpit and rushed down the aisle straight to Mildred. He welcomed her—as other people were also gathering around to welcome her.

Everyone was so nice and caring! Mildred broke down crying—sobbing profusely. Then everyone, putting their arms around her, asked why she was crying. What's wrong?

In between her sobs, Mildred told them that God had taken her husband and left her with two little boys to care for and raise all alone—and that her husband was up in heaven with God looking down on her and *not helping her at all.*

Immediately, the different people started telling her the truth of what the Bible says, each one telling her a different part:

"God is love," one said (1 John 4:8).

"Your husband is NOT up there with God; Roy is sleeping until Jesus comes back," added another.

"Oh, no honey, your husband is not up in heaven with Jesus; he is in the ground or wherever his body was placed. He's not in heaven. Man made that up. That idea is NOT from God."

Then someone else said, "For everything God says in the Bible, Satan has a counterfeit. Satan makes people believe that when you die you go to heaven or hell. But God says in His Word: 'For the living know that they shall die, but the dead know not anything'" (Eccles. 9:5, 6).

Mildred said to me, "They opened their Bibles, and showed me right there and then that what they were telling me is the truth, straight from the Bible. It was so opposite from what my pastor and friends had told me! It was beautiful and so full of hope—I just loved it! They showed me so many verses of promise!" Here are a few of them:

> God says: "For the wages of sin is death; but the gift of God is eternal life through Jesus Christ our Lord" (Rom. 6:23). But Satan's lie says: "Ye shall not surely die" (Gen. 3:4).

> God says: "The soul that sinneth, it shall die" (Ezek. 18:20).

> God is the only one who is immortal: "Which in his times He shall shew, who is the blessed and only Potentate, the King of kings, and Lord of lords; Who ONLY hath immortality..." (1 Timothy 6:15, 16, emphasis added).

> OUR immortality will come at Christ's second coming: "Behold, I shew you a mystery; We shall not all sleep, but we shall all be changed, In a moment, in the twinkling of an eye, at the last trump: for the trumpet shall sound, and the dead shall be raised incorruptible, and

we shall be changed. For this corruptible must put on incorruption, and this **mortal** must put on immortality. So when this corruptible shall have put on incorruption, and this **mortal** shall have put on immortality, then shall be brought to pass the saying that is written, Death is swallowed up in victory. O death, where is thy sting? O grave, where is thy victory?" (1 Cor. 15:51–55).

Christ died so sinners need not perish (die permanently): "For God so loved the world, that he gave his only begotten Son, that whosoever believeth in him should not perish, but have everlasting life" (John 3:16).

Our spirit (which is our breath) returns to God when we die: "Then shall the dust return to the earth as it was: and the spirit shall return unto God who gave it" (Eccles. 12:7). What this means is that Body + Breath= Living Soul (Gen. 2:7).

The dead are unconscious: "For the living know that they shall die: but the dead know not any thing, neither have they any more a reward; for the memory of them is forgotten. Also their love, and their hatred, and their envy, is now perished; neither have they any more a portion for ever in any thing that is done under the sun" (Eccles. 9:5, 6).

Another church member said, "No, honey, Roy isn't looking down on you and watching you suffer. He doesn't even know you are suffering—he couldn't stand to see you having such a hard time; you know that."

Our thoughts perish at death: "His breath goeth forth, he returneth to his earth; in that very day his thoughts perish" (Ps. 146:4).

Mildred also told me, "When Roy died, he no longer knew anything about me or the boys! 'His sons come to honour, and he knoweth it not; and they are brought low, but he perceiveth it not of them' (Job 14:21). Oh, WOW, that was such a relief to know! I had actually started hating Roy because I thought he was up there having fun and watching me suffer.

"Soon after he died, Roy started appearing to me at night. He would be at the foot of my bed , telling me peaceful, loving things—like he was trying to comfort me. But it was all so scary to me. It wasn't peaceful at all. It was like he was lying to me because it didn't help anything. It didn't help my bruised hands; it didn't help our little boys to have enough food to eat; it didn't stop them from wondering why he left them in the first place.

"In reading and showing me these Bible texts, one of the church members showed me Job 7:10, which told me he doesn't even return to his house: "He shall return no more to his house, neither shall his place know him any more."

"That was a relief, too—to know that wasn't really Roy at the foot of my bed at night telling me things. It was actually Satan's angels, spirits of the devils, sprits of the occult appearing as Roy. 'For they are the spirits of devils, working miracles, which go forth unto the kings of the earth and of the whole world'" (Rev. 16:14).

Jesus even calls death a sleep—just like when we close our eyes at night—we don't know anything until we wake up. "These things said he: and after that he saith unto them, Our friend Lazarus sleepeth; but I go, that I may awake him out of sleep ... Then said Jesus unto them plainly, Lazarus is dead" (John 11:11, 14).

Happily, Mildred said to me "Roy is sleeping—he knows *nothing* of what I'm going through, then or now. He will wake up when Jesus comes and we will all be together again, as a happy family—if I and the boys are faithful. 'Marvel not at this: for the hour is coming, in the which all that are in the graves shall hear his voice, And shall come forth; they that have done good, unto the resurrection of life; and they that have done evil, unto the resurrection of damnation'" (John 5:28, 29).

Mildred said, "I just loved learning this, and I love knowing it now. It's so loving and peaceful. I have not for a moment hated Roy or God anymore. I love God now more than ever.

"I especially love 1 Thessalonians 4:13–18: 'But I would not have you to be ignorant, brethren, concerning them which are asleep, that ye sorrow not, even as others which have no hope. For if we believe that Jesus died and rose again, even so them also which sleep in Jesus will God bring with him [to heaven]. For this we say unto you by the word of the Lord, that we which are alive and remain unto the coming of the Lord shall not prevent them which are asleep. For the Lord himself shall descend from heaven with a shout, with the voice of the archangel, and with the trump of God: and the dead in Christ shall rise first: Then we which are alive and remain shall be caught up together with them in the clouds, to meet the Lord in the air: and so shall we ever be with the Lord. Wherefore comfort one another with these words.'"

Listening to these people and seeing it for herself in the Bible, Mildred stopped crying. She had never heard such beautiful truths before! She said to me, "I had never read the Bible for myself. I always just believed whatever my pastor and elder told me."

"The lady that kept holding my hand, the minister that had rushed to me, and the people who kept coming over were so kind to me! One man hired me right on the spot to work in his office as his secretary in the daytime, and he would train me. Another lady said, 'I will come to your apartment and take care of your little boys while you work, and you don't have to pay me, because I am retired and get my monthly check; my children are grown and I love little boys.'"

Mildred was so happily overwhelmed that she started crying again—this time with joy.

Mildred told me, "Through all of these years, I have always believed that Jesus or an angel helped me to hear that beautiful music from that church so far away—over all the traffic, horns, and noise of the city streets."

Heavenly Music

from Hymns of God's peculiar people, by James White, 1849

from Hymns and Tunes, 1886

♩ = 100

1. What heavenly music steals o-ver the sea! Entrancing the senses like sweet melody! 'Tis the voice of the angels borne soft on the air; For me they are singing; their welcome I hear.
2. On the banks of old Jordan, here gazing I stand, And earnestly longing, I stretch forth my hand; Send a convoy of angels, dear Jesus, I pray! Let me join that sweet music; come, take me away.
3. Though dark are the waters and rough is the wave, If Jesus permit, the wild surges I'll brave; For that heavenly music hath ravished me so, I must join in that chorus! I'll go, let me go!

Mia

As I relate the story that Mildred told me, I am reminded of another lady that I met some years later.

Mia had just moved into our area and started coming to our church in Arden, North Carolina. You couldn't help but notice that she was always helping people, and she was always smiling and happy. I just loved her. No matter what kind of a day I had, looking at her and watching her always perked me up.

One day I drove into a driveway to visit an elderly couple that turned out not to be at home, but I knew they would be back soon, so I decided to wait for them. Right then, this "happy lady," Mia, pulled into the same driveway right up beside me. She, too, was coming to visit the couple. She decided to wait for them also.

> *"I love your smile, your laugh, and your happy attitude. How is it that you are always happy?"*

Mia and I stood beside our cars talking. I couldn't help myself, I just had to ask, "I love your smile, your laugh, and your happy attitude. How is it that you are *always* happy?" This is what she told me:

"I used to live out west in the desert with my husband and three children. We were not Christians—I knew nothing of God. My youngest child, my precious little four-year-old daughter caught a disease and died.

"Six years later, my sixteen-year-old son and his friends had found a cave up in the mountains behind our house, there in the desert. They spent most of their free time up there. My son had moved a couple of our extra arm chairs and other useful things up to their cave to make it more comfortable. They loved it up there. One day, our son didn't come home for dinner. My husband walked up the mountain to the cave to tell the boys it was time to eat. He found nothing but a big hole of sand. The cave had fallen in! In desperation, he started digging and calling. He found our son—dead! Our son's face was only four inches from air—from the top of the sand. Because we didn't know God, it devastated both of us—especially, my husband, who died six months later from the grief and anguish."

Soon after that, Mia attended some evangelistic meetings and learned about God and Jesus and their love for her. She and her other daughter gave their hearts to the Lord. As Mia told the details, I was standing there crying, thinking of all of this. All she had left now was her middle child, her other daughter, now, years later, grown and living in another state.

I was standing there with watery eyes for all her sadness, when suddenly she briskly started patting my arm and *very* excitedly said, "So, see now what I have to look forward to in the resurrection?! That's why I'm ALWAYS happy—I can't wait until Jesus comes and wakes up my precious family—daughter, son, and husband—so we can be together again FOREVER!"

So THAT was why Mia was always happy. Her mind stayed continually on her future with Jesus, and the resurrection. WOW! What a way to get through her trials! Such a good example for me—for all of us—to get through our trials. We, too, can choose to keep OUR minds on Jesus and look forward to OUR future with Him.

"Thou wilt keep him in perfect *peace*, whose mind is *stayed* on thee: because he trusteth in thee" (Isa. 26:3, emphasis added).

Bulgaria

One Wednesday morning, there was a knock on my door. When I opened it, there stood my pastor. After greetings, he said, "I want you to go to Bulgaria with me to conduct evangelistic meetings."

I said, "Wow! I'd love to go." I would be very happy to HELP HIM with the meetings. "But, uh, I don't have any money."

The pastor said, "Well, pray about it." And left.

Three days later, on Sabbath morning, in the foyer of the church, the pastor came up to me and said, "Have you been praying?"

I answered, "Yes, but I still don't have any money."

He said, "We-e-e-ll, there is a family willing to pay your airline ticket."

Surprised, I almost shouted, "Wow, that's great!"

Then he continued, "And there's another family willing to pay all of your expenses."

By then, my mouth was hanging wide open in astonishment. At that moment, another friend came from across the foyer and said to me, "I understand you would like to go on this mission trip, but you can't afford to miss work."

I said, "Well, that's true!" (I'm one of those people who lives from paycheck to paycheck.)

This person, evidently knowing already that the mission trip was for three weeks, said, "How much would you make in that three weeks?" I told him, and he replied, "Well consider that paid too!"

WOW! I couldn't believe it! God definitely wanted me in Bulgaria! We were leaving in two weeks, and, as I prepared for the trip, I found out that I was NOT helping the pastor with his meetings; I was going to be preaching myself through an interpreter. That really scared me. I knew absolutely *nothing* about preaching, and especially in front of actual, *real, live people!* I was crying one day when my daughter called from where she was in graduate school. I told her, as I was sobbing, "Oh, Katy, I don't know what I've gotten myself into!"

She replied, very sternly, "Mother, you haven't gotten yourself into anything. God got you into it and He will carry you through it. So, stop your blubbering."

"Oh, yes, she's right," I thought. *"God knows all about preaching in front of real, live people."*

One day, soon after this conversation, my little nine-year-old granddaughter, Rachel, called and said, "Grandma, I know something that will help you in Bulgaria."

Thinking it would be a cute little child's idea, I said, "What is it, honey?"

She said, "What God said to Moses: 'I will be with thy mouth and teach thee what thou shalt say'" (Exod. 4:12).

Wow, that was super!

Yes, of course, this was God's doing, not mine. He will do this *through* me, not because of me.

Another Bible verse someone else told me is: "And all this assembly shall know that the Lord saveth not with sword and spear: for the battle is the Lord's, and he will give you into our hands" (1 Sam. 17:47).

Also, "But the LORD said unto me, ... thou shalt go to all that I shall send thee, and whatsoever I command thee thou shalt speak. *Be not afraid of their faces:* for I am with thee to deliver thee, saith the LORD. ... the LORD said unto me, Behold, I have put my words in thy mouth" (Jer. 1:7–9, emphasis added).

On the plane flying to Bulgaria, God impressed me to pray, "Help me love these people where I am going like You do." Actually, that's something I've been praying ever since, in all kinds of situations that involve other people. "God, help me love them like You do." It works without exception.

Back to Bulgaria, though. God's words through little Rachel came to my mind and helped me through *every* sermon. God preached nineteen sermons through me. He worked on hearts. He convicted. He did everything! My interpreter and I were basically the only English speakers in the whole auditorium, although there was one lady that spoke a little English from visiting the States.

On the third night, a lady came up to me and said through my interpreter, "Please pray for my son, Daveed. He is very mean."

I said, "How old is your son?"

She answered, "Seven."

I thought, oh my, just how mean can a seven-year-old be?

She continued, "He hits and kicks the other children in school. He's very mean to the teacher. He tears up the desks, walls, and other things at school."

I replied, "Yes, I will pray for him, but *you bring him* to these meetings."

Horrified, she said, "No, no—he would tear up everything and hurt the people!!"

I said, "YOU BRING HIM to the meetings!"

The next night, as the people were gathering in the small auditorium, in through the main door walked the distressed mother and a little broad-shouldered seven-year-old boy in a black leather jacket, walking like he owned the world. Quickly, I ran over to him, leaned over, and greeted him the Bulgarian way, a kiss on each cheek, as I said, "Oh, Daveed, I'm *so* glad to meet you! *So* glad you came!" He gave me a huge smile.

I said, "Come over here; I want to tell you a story." He, along with the interpreter, went with me to the other side of the auditorium, away from all the talking people. He listened intently to the children's story that I told him. At the end of it I asked, "Daveed, do you know who Jesus is?"

He shook his head. I said as I pointed up, "Well, Jesus lives in heaven and He loves you very much and He wants you to be a good boy."

Leading him to the front of the auditorium, I took him to a seat right in front of the projector screen. I said, "You sit right here and you will see a picture of Jesus, the One who loves you so much!"

Daveed came to the meetings every single night after that and always sat in the front. One night when his mother could not come, Daveed convinced his Communist grandmother to bring him. She enjoyed it, too!

After about two weeks of the meetings, Daveed came up to me and said, "I didn't hit anybody in school today."

I bubbled over as I hugged him and said, "I am so very proud of you." Then, I continued happily, "And Jesus is very proud of you, too." Daveed just beamed.

I found out that one of the reasons for the meanness in this little boy was that his dad, mother, and he lived with Communist grandparents, who, before this, never allowed any talk of Jesus, Christianity, nor prayer in their home. Hence, he had only known severe discipline without the love of God.

A few nights later, Daveed's mother drew me aside after our meeting and, very frightened, said, "Daveed's school teacher called me today."

I said, "Oh, really! What did she say?"

His mother answered, "She was very loud, yelling at me."

Communism had just supposedly fallen in those Eastern European countries. Although even the Bulgarian president and many of the leaders and head people were still communists, they could supposedly not enforce it, but the people still had their fears, reasonably. This mother was bodily shaking as she related the happenings of that day to me.

In an angry-sounding voice Daveed's still-Communist teacher demanded to know, "What has happened to Daveed?! What has happened to Daveed?! He is kind to me and the children now!" And again, in strong words, "What has happened to him? I want to know what YOU have done!"

A few nights later, Daveed's mother drew me aside after our meeting and, very frightened, said, "Daveed's school teacher called me today"

This meek and shaking mother was so frightened that she was scared to tell the angry teacher. She stayed silent on her end of the phone until the teacher kept demanding SO strongly.

Finally, this little, brave mother spoke. She answered softly, "Daveed is attending some Christian meetings with me—learning about Jesus and how Jesus wants him to be a good boy."

Stone silence reigned on the other end of the phone while the little mother shook and fought back tears. Finally, after several moments, the teacher said, more calmly, "Oh," and hung up.

That little mother came to our meetings that night extremely frightened, not knowing what would happen next. God impressed the words on me right then, as I smiled big and hugged her snuggly to stop her shaking. I said, convincingly, "Just look how Daveed's conversion can influence even his teacher. We will pray that the other children will see Jesus in your son, and tell their parents, and also that his Communist teacher will see Jesus, and all will come to our Lord before it's too late. Isn't that exciting?!"

The mother quit shaking, and as she thought about God's possibilities for a moment, she began to smile. Then she got excited, and we prayed right there that God would bring that to pass.

The whole congregation lined up at the entrance to shake our hands as they left every night, and my translator and I shook each hand and always said, "God bless you; see you tomorrow night." There were other exits, but to our delight, each person wanted to personally greet us. I loved it!

* * *

In the congregation was another lady who always came early and sat on the second row. There was also a man that always came just as we started the meeting and sat in the back. One evening, someone informed me that they were husband and wife, but she had become a Seventh-day Adventist Christian and he was still a Communist and made fun of her, so they didn't get along. The next night, when the big, tall Communist husband—I'll call him Ivan—took my hand, I asked, "Where is your wife?"

He looked back down the long line of people behind him and thrust his hand that way, saying, "Back there somewhere." Then, frowning and shaking his head, he continued, "We don't get along."

I said, smiling, "Well, I'll pray about that!"

Looking kind of whimsically at me, he said, "Oh, that won't do any good!"

I responded, "Well, I'll pray anyway," as he laughingly left the auditorium.

> *Ivan gave Pavla a big kiss and looked at me and said, "We get along now." Then pointing up toward God, this Communist man said, "He did it"*

Each night, the wife—I'll call her Pavla—continued to come alone and sit on the second row, while Ivan still came later and sat in the back. I continued to pray for them privately—then one night they both came into the meeting together and sat in the middle of the auditorium, not in the front, and not in the back.

After the meeting, they came through line together, holding hands. Stopping right in front of me, Ivan gave Pavla a big kiss and looked at me and said, "We get along now." Then pointing up toward God, this Communist man said, "He did it."

God is so *awesome!* He can change *any* heart—even mine and yours, dear Reader, if we will only let Him. "In all thy ways acknowledge him, and he shall direct thy paths" (Prov. 3:6).

* * *

Though Communism had fallen, the people were still afraid to trust. Over here in America, when there are evangelistic meetings, cards are handed out to see who would like more information on the topics presented, or a visit from the evangelist, or prayer for something. Over in the now fallen Communist countries, back then, when I was conducting these meetings, you couldn't hand out cards. The untrusting people would not give their addresses or any information at all to anyone. Understandably they refused to share that with me, too; I had heard the stories of what all they had been through.

They told me that, during the rule of Communism, there would be a Communist official standing at the door of any Christian church and whoever entered, maybe for Christmas or Easter, their name was written down. Then the next morning they either lost their job, were imprisoned, or were killed.

So, knowing not to ask for addresses or information, one night God impressed me to handout papers and ask for just their names and a conviction, by writing only their name and putting a little cross in the upper right hand comer, so I could pray for them using their name. Someone found some sheets of typing paper and we tore them in fourths to make enough to hand out to everyone. Then we found a few pencils to share.

We had just studied the seventh day Sabbath, emphasizing Bible verses such as:

1. Genesis 2:2, 3 tells us that the Sabbath was instituted at Creation. "And on the seventh day God ended his work which he had made; and he rested on the seventh day from all his work which he had made. And God blessed the seventh day, and sanctified it: because that in it he had rested from all his work which God created and made."
2. We rest in honor of our Creator. Exodus 20:8, 11 reminds us to, "Remember the sabbath day, to keep it holy. ... For in six days the Lord made heaven and earth, the sea, and all that in them is, and rested the seventh day: wherefore the Lord blessed the sabbath day, and hallowed it."

3. Ezekiel 20:12 tells us that the Sabbath is also a sign of God's sanctifying power. "Moreover also I gave them my sabbaths, to be a sign between me and them, that they might know that I am the Lord that sanctify them."
4. We also learned that if our God in heaven has the power to make something as intangible as a day, holy, then He surely has the power to make a person holy. Sabbath was made for mankind—not just for the Jews. Jesus is Lord of the Sabbath. Mark 2:27, 28 says, "And he said unto them, The sabbath was made for man, and not man for the sabbath: Therefore the Son of man is Lord also of the sabbath."
5. Jesus' custom was to keep the Sabbath. We learn in Luke 4:16: "And he came to Nazareth, where he had been brought up: and, as his custom was, he went into the synagogue on the sabbath day, and stood up for to read."
6. In Matthew 24:15–20 Jesus shares that He expected His followers to still be keeping the Sabbath at the fall of Jerusalem, nearly forty years after His death. "When ye therefore shall see the abomination of desolation, spoken of by Daniel the prophet, stand in the holy place, (whoso readeth, let him understand:) Then let them which be in Judaea flee into the mountains: Let him which is on the housetop not come down to take any thing out of his house: Neither let him which is in the field return back to take his clothes. And woe unto them that are with child, and to them that give suck in those days! But pray ye that your flight be not in the winter, neither on the sabbath day:"
7. Isaiah 66:22, 23 tells us that the Sabbath will be kept in the new earth. "For as the new heavens and the new earth, which I will make, shall remain before me, saith the Lord, so shall your seed and your name remain. And it shall come to pass, that from one new moon to another, and from one sabbath to another, shall all flesh come to worship before me, saith the Lord."
8. In Luke 23:54–56 we learn that the Sabbath day followed the crucifixion. "And that day was the preparation, and the sabbath drew on. And the women also, which came with him from Galilee, followed after, and beheld the sepulchre, and how his body was laid. And they returned, and prepared spices and ointments; and rested the sabbath day according to the commandment."
9. God's commandment in Exodus 20:10 forbids work on Sabbath: "But the seventh day is the sabbath of the Lord thy God: in it

thou shalt not do any work, thou, nor thy son, nor thy daughter, thy manservant, nor thy maidservant, nor thy cattle, nor thy stranger that is within thy gates:"
10. Luke 24:1 illustrates that the Sabbath is followed by the first day of the week: "Now upon the first day of the week, very early in the morning, they came unto the sepulchre, bringing the spices which they had prepared, and certain others with them."
11. Most Christians recognize that Jesus was crucified and died on Good Friday and rose on Easter Sunday. *The Sabbath is the day between*—a time to pause, rest, and keep our mind on our Creator, Jesus.

Obedience is the evidence of love.
"If ye love me, keep my commandments" (John 14:15).

So, with God's guidance, I asked that whoever wants to show God they love Him and wants to totally obey Him by keeping His Sabbath day to write their name and draw a little cross in the corner. There were no ushers, so different people picked them up and brought them to me. *Every single person* in the auditorium that night signed a paper and put a cross in the corner! I held the whole pack of papers representing convictions up toward heaven and prayed right then and there for all those precious people. I know God will save them. They had nothing of this world's goods, but they had found Jesus, which is everything.

* * *

In that audience there were five teenage boys that came every night and sat together. During the course of the meetings, I found out that they rode a train for *two hours* and then rode a bus across town to the auditorium to these meetings each and every night, and then rode that same distance back to their home after the meeting.

There were also twelve-year-old twins, a boy and a girl, that came every night and sat on the front row. Their parents never came, but the twins were always there. Many, many, many precious souls were won for the kingdom.

In the United States, sometimes during evangelistic meetings the attendance drops, but not over there. We started out with forty-one people coming to the meetings. On the last night, when I prayerfully made the appeal asking who wanted to obey God and live with Him forever in heaven and the earth made new, seventy-one people came forward.

"For the Lamb which is in the midst of the throne shall feed them, and shall lead them unto living fountains of waters: and God shall wipe away all tears from their eyes" (Rev. 7:17).

The last night's theme was heaven, and I told them about the river of life (Rev. 22:1) and asked if we could all meet at the tree of life someday (Rev. 22:2). I told them that we could meet beside the tree on the first Sabbath. They all agreed. We talked about all being there, with no one missing. I was crying, along with the whole audience. We had all fallen in love with each other through Jesus. He had brought us all into one accord.

"Fulfil ye my joy, that ye be likeminded, having the same love, being of one accord, of one mind" (Phil. 2:2).

I grew to dearly love each one of those people and I pray for them still today. I told them that I am up early every morning to pray and study my Bible and that I will be praying for them at that time. That turns out to be 11:00 each morning for them, so they *know* that at 11:00 each morning their time I will be praying for them. Many told me that they will stop and pray for me at that time, too. I am so thankful.

> *We had all fallen in love with each other through Jesus. He had brought us all into one accord*

There were twenty-six that asked for baptism right then. Several others asked for more Bible studies. See how God came through with His promises: "Now therefore go, and I will be with thy mouth, and teach thee what thou shalt say" (Exod. 4:12), and "Be not afraid nor dismayed by reason of this great multitude; for the battle is not yours, but God's" (2 Chron. 20:15). Also, "But the Lord said unto me, Say not, I am a child: for thou shalt go to all that I shall send thee, and whatsoever I command thee thou shalt speak. Be not afraid of their faces: for I am with thee to deliver thee, saith the Lord. Then the Lord put forth his hand, and touched my mouth. And the Lord said unto me, Behold, I have put My words in thy mouth" (Jer. 1:7–9).

I have heard it said, "We are not to be in the world as Christ's witnesses, but we are to be in Christ as witnesses to the world." God used this scared and blubbering child of His to accomplish His work, and helped me to love like He does, as He told me to pray. The Bible tells us that Jesus even used fishermen for His purpose. I don't even know how to fish, but He still used me, because, "with God nothing shall be impossible" (Luke 1:37). Wow! What a mighty God we serve!

"How then shall they call on him in whom they have not believed? and how shall they believe in him of whom they have not heard? and how shall they hear without a preacher? And how shall they preach, except they be sent? as it is written, How beautiful are the feet of them that preach the gospel of peace, and bring glad tidings of good things!" (Rom. 10:14, 15).

The "Angel" in White

I was driving to my daddy's place in Tennessee to pick up my daughter, Katy. She had spent a week with him and Granny. It was a five-hour trip. I was driving from North Carolina on I-40 to the turnoff to go south to Daddy's. There was still another hour-and-a-half to go, so I knew I could get to his place before dark.

Suddenly, going seventy mph, the car slowed and stopped. I managed to ease over onto the shoulder to get out of the rushing traffic. Hard as I tried to restart the motor, it wouldn't start. Fighting off tears, I sat there praying. Then all of a sudden the car started. I drove to the exit, got off, and started down the two-lane road to Daddy's. Suddenly the car slowed and stopped again. I repeated my prayer and finally it started. I saw a policeman at the next service station. With my hopes encouraged, I whipped into the station to ask the policeman where to get help. I told him my story and waited to see what he recommended.

Sarcastically, he said, "You got a cell phone?"

I said, "Yes, sir."

He said, "Well, use it." And drove off.

I had no knowledge of that town, and I was not able to look up anything on my old flip-phone.

I thought, "Well, I know how to get gas." So while I was at the station, I filled the tank up with gas. The car started right up and I continued my journey. But, at the outskirts of that town, the car stopped again. By now, I was thinking it must be the fuel pump. Years before, this same thing had happened to another car that my husband was driving. But now that I had come to this conclusion, what do I do and where do I go?

I decided I had better not leave the town and get out in the country where there would be no mechanics at all. The next time the car started I turned it around and started back toward town. As I came into the city limits, the car stopped again. After sitting on a very narrow shoulder for about ten minutes, a car pulled up behind me. A lady got out and came to my window and asked if she could help.

I told her my dilemma and she said, "I know where there's a car parts place. Follow me and I'll take you there."

So I followed her. Bless her heart! She had a carload of children, but still watched out the rear-view mirror and when my car would stop, she would pull over and wait.

Finally, we pulled into the parking lot of a car parts store. I parked, got out, and ran to her car to thank her and to give the children some little booklets of children's stories. After we talked, she left and I went into the store.

I told the man behind the counter my story and asked what he thought it could be. He claimed he didn't know, so I said, "It might be the fuel pump." So he checked the make and model of the car and took a fuel pump off the shelf. Then he informed me that you can't put a fuel pump on without a certain tool. Believing him, I also paid for that tool.

He also said, "You will lose all your gasoline when it is changed, too."

I thought, "Oh, dear! I just filled up, and now I will have to buy another tank of gas." I said, "Can you or someone here put it on for me?"

He said "no," not offering any more information.

I asked, "Where would a garage be where I could get it put on?"

Looking at his watch, he said, sarcastically, "It's 4:30; no one in this town would start that big job at this hour. Every place closes at 5:00. It would take too long. But they open at 8:00 in the morning; then they would fix it."

I said, "But, I'm from out of town and I don't have any place to stay."

He said, "Oh, I'll let you sleep in our parking lot. The cops won't bother you."

Ready to cry again, I quickly took my fuel pump and tool and went out the door. There, sitting in the parking lot was another policeman. Hopes up again, I ran over to him and asked for help. He, too, was belligerent, and answered the same way after hearing my story. "You can sleep here in this parking lot tonight. I'll tell the other guys so they'll leave you alone."

I made it to the safety of my own car before I started crying. After a while, whatever bravery I had left returned, and I decided to head for Daddy's even if it took all night to get there (starting and stopping).

I couldn't remember all the turns we had taken from the highway to the auto parts store. So, I just started driving. Surely, I would get out of this unfriendly town eventually!

The car slowed and stopped once again and I drifted onto some gravel off of the road. Sitting there crying wasn't helping anything, so I decided to do something. One thing I know how to do for a motor is put oil in it. The other thing I know is how to change a tire, but obviously that didn't have anything to do with this. I got out of the car. It was dark by now, so I left the headlights on so I could see a little bit. I finally got the hood raised (that was another challenge we won't discuss at this time). I always carried a quart of oil, so I got it out of the trunk. I took the lid off the oil fill place on the motor and the lid off the oil container.

I was just starting to tip the container up when a big pickup truck pulled up behind my car. A man got out and came walking toward me from the back of the car. My hood was up; he couldn't see from where he was what I was doing on the other side of the hood. But he said in a deep voice, "Don't put oil in it." How did he know what I was doing?

I stopped and didn't pour anything. He came up to me, dressed in white, super-clean coveralls. He pointed to a place across the way where there was a paved parking lot and the businesses were closed, so no cars were there, and said, "Drive your car over there where it's paved."

He put my hood down, I got into my car, and drove over there with him following. I stopped in the middle of the parking lot and he drove around to the front of the car. I got out and stood there.

This man not only was dressed totally in white, including his shoes, but his huge pickup was totally white and very clean. In the back of the truck were only three things: a ramp to drive my car up on, a huge cardboard-like mat for him to lie on, and a pair of white gloves. The man got the ramp out of his truck, laid it on the ground in front of my car, and told me to drive up on it, which I did. Then I got out of my car and stood there, not knowing what else to do.

He slid the big mat under the car, put his white gloves on, and lay down face up on the mat and slid under the car. He worked under there for a few short minutes then reached his hand out toward me and said, "May I have the new fuel pump?" I handed it to him and asked if he needed the tool. He said "no."

In another short time, he slid out from under the car. He said, "I'm sorry, I lost a drop of your gas."

I said, "Oh, that's okay—I just appreciate you changing the pump." I remembered the parts man saying how messy it would be, that I would lose most of my gas, and that it would take a longer time than anyone would want to do that time of day. From the time this nice man slid under the car until he came back out was less than fifteen minutes, and his gloves were still totally white, with not one smudge on them.

I thanked him, but he wouldn't let me pay him. He said, "Drive down this road and pull over into the Wal-Mart parking lot and see if your car drives okay, and I will follow you." So I did. When I got there, he pulled up beside me in his truck, and said, "Run okay?"

I said, "Yes."

He said "good," and drove away.

Even if he wasn't a white coverall-clad angel, he was definitely sent by God. I finished my trip safely. God is so *awesome!*

I thought it was interesting, and the similarities were more than coincidence, that the Bible tells us that God gave Gideon only three things to accomplish the work that needed to be done in the battle situation that he was facing: a trumpet, a pitcher, and a torch (Judges 7:16–23).

God gave this man in white only three tools to use to do what God knew had to be done for my situation: a ramp, a mat to lie on, and white gloves to protect his hands. (Or were they to show the cleanliness of a normally messy job?) This shows that God is with us today, just like He was with the people in the Bible stories with which we are all familiar.

"I sought the Lord; and He heard me, and delivered me from all my fears" (Ps. 34:4).

Thoughts

"In the multitude of my thoughts within me thy comforts delight my soul" (Ps. 94:19).

I am sitting here looking out over the ocean, observing the strength of the mighty waves. They swell to monstrous size—big and blue—then crash into big white billows of foam across the shoreline.

The sky above is deep blue as far as I can see, meeting the vast ocean way over at the horizon; the white billowy clouds drifting across the sky match the ocean foam. The trees swaying in the breeze, the flowers nodding to their Creator God, and the colorful birds flying through the air and singing their beautiful songs, always on key, paint a picture of every peaceful color that is beautiful to the eye.

And thinking about what's under those waves, every color pleasing to the eye is also down there: fluorescent orange starfish, green and purple anemone, red lobsters, yellow crabs, gorgeous fish, underwater plants—even aquatic animals that sing!

But back to the waves! Oh, what do you know?! The waves are still swelling and crashing.

They didn't stop just because I forgot to keep thinking about them and was thinking about the sky instead. And the clouds didn't drop out of the sky because I forgot them momentarily and was thinking about the birds. Everything God made is good and it all works in unison in spite of me and what I am doing or thinking!

Wouldn't it be terrible if God decided not to think of me today because I didn't think of Him? It would be horrible if one day God said, "Rita didn't think of Me; she didn't spend time with Me when she got up this morning, so I won't let the sun rise over her." Or, "I will keep the birds asleep so they won't sing for her today, and she won't have daylight today, only darkness, because she didn't spend time thinking of Me."

As mighty as God is, running the whole universe, keeping everything in its place and turning or moving, rotating or twinkling, He still thinks of us—little ol' me, and little ol' you. In fact, it is because He IS thinking of us that He keeps all of this going ... because He does think of us and loves us "the mostest."

He wants us to think of Him, to love Him enough to obey Him, because He loves us. Yes, He's mighty! Mighty enough to save even me, if I will let Him. Mighty enough to save even you, if you will let Him. He rules the universe, and yet cares enough to live in our hearts! That is *awesome!*

"Casting all your care upon him; for he careth for you" (1 Pet. 5:7).

I Sing the Almighty Power of God

1. I sing the mighty power of God that made the mountians rise,
   that spread the flowing seas abroad and built the lofty skies.
   I sing the wisdom that ordained the sun to rule the day;
   the moon shines full at his command and all the stars obey.

2. I sing the goodness of the Lord that filled the earth with food;
   he formed the creatures with his word and then pronounced them good.
   Lord, how your wonders are displayed wher-e'er I turn my eye,
   if I survey the ground I tread or gaze upon the sky!

3. There's not a plant or flower below but makes your glories known,
   and clouds arise and tempests blow by order from your throne;
   while all that borrows life from you is ever in your care,
   and everywhere that we can be, you, God, are present there.

Text: Isaac Watts (1674-1748)
Tune: *Gesangbuch der H. W. K. Hofkapelle*, 1784

CMD
ELLACOMBE
www.hymnary.org/text/i_sing_the_mighty_power_of_god

This hymn is in the public domain. You may freely use this score for personal and congregational worship. If you reproduce the score, please credit Hymnary.org as the source.

Life After Cancer Cure

While serving in World War II, my daddy, Amos Enoch Crowder, had been stabbed in the stomach. The consequences were severely ongoing, and finally, after ten years of hemorrhaging and constant pain, the doctor took all but one-fifth of his stomach out. The doctor told him at that time, "Amos, now you will have to eat meat every single day. Fruits and vegetables digest in four or five hours; they go straight through you like they are supposed to. But now, you have to keep something in your stomach, and since meat takes 24–48 hours to digest, you must have some every day."

So, all of my life my daddy ate meat. Every time he tried to get off of it, he would end up in the hospital almost dead. I have horrible memories from my childhood of coming home from school to find my daddy lying on the floor, having just fallen, unconscious, with Mother rushing in to him.

Therefore, many years later, when Daddy, at age eighty-six, came to live with me in my home, I knew immediately that he would need his meat to survive. By this time I had gone totally vegan (no animal products, plus I gave up refined foods, too). I ate only fruits, grains, nuts, seeds, and vegetables. Daddy had been battling cancer for eight years. He had already had four cancer surgeries and had lost to surgery half of his left ear and all of his lymph nodes down the left side of his neck, into his shoulder and chest. But the cancer kept coming back.

> *"Do you think this meat is causing my cancer?"*

One day while we were eating at the dining room table, Daddy looked at his plate of "country style steak," one of his favorites. Then he looked over at my plate of vegetables and said, pointing to his plate, "Do you think this meat is causing my cancer?"

I said, "Yes," because I remembered what a doctor had told me years before, that meat sits in the colon for many hours, comes to body temperature, and putrefies. Then, whatever chemicals or diseases are in that meat are absorbed into our blood stream, causing diseases in us.

Daddy said, "Well, I want to quit."

Thinking of my childhood memories of Daddy unconscious on the floor, I said, sternly, "No, Daddy!"

He said, "Yes. This is my last meat!"

I was so scared! Before this, Mother had been here to help Daddy. Now, she was dead, and his care was up to me—that really frightened me!

Since Daddy was so determined to get off his meat, I said, "Okay, Daddy, but only with prayer."

Right then, Daddy and I held hands, and I prayed, "God, if it is your will that Daddy get off of meat, then please, don't let him get sick anymore."

Well, God, as you know, doesn't just halfway do something! Not only did Daddy not ever get sick from not eating meat anymore, but he never had another sniffle, cold, or anything! Daddy went totally vegan right there on the spot and was "healthy as a horse" from then on.

Since it was already scheduled, and since I didn't know what all was going on in his body, I went ahead and took Daddy for his next cancer surgery six weeks later. The woman doctor didn't totally put him to sleep because of his advanced age, so he was groggy during the procedure, but aware. She worked, and looked, and looked, and worked. Finally, out loud to the nurse, she said, "Well, it's got to be in here somewhere" (meaning the cancer that she had found earlier).

In his groggy state, Daddy said slowly, "No-o-o, it do-es-n't."

Surprised, the doctor looked at him and said, "Why not?"

Daddy said, groggily, "My dau–ght–er is giv-ing–me–raw–vege–tables."

The doctor had never heard of such a thing, and because she hadn't found any cancer, she stopped the surgery. After cleaning up, she came to me, and said, "What's this about raw vegetables? Your daddy's cancer is gone!"

I explained how Daddy had quit eating all animal products, including meat, fish, dairy, cheese, eggs, and refined foods like white flour and white sugar. We only eat fruits, vegetables, whole grains, and nuts.

The surgeon did not know about all of this, and said, "That sounds really good and healthy. I want to start doing that, too."

I told her how I packed three types of raw greens—say turnip, kale, and collards—in the blender with a little juice (Daddy liked apple juice or white grape peach juice, so one or the other). After it is blended to total liquid, then I finish filling the blender with the same juice and blend smooth. Daddy would drink a whole glass and sometimes the whole blender full once a day before his midday meal. Any other raw vegetable that he couldn't chew would be put in the blender, too, like lettuce and other raw salad vegetables, when we had that type of salad, so he could get all the nutrients.

Guests that came to eat with us loved this "green drink," too. Sometimes I would end up making four blenders full at one meal for every one of our visitors to drink.

When I was a child, Mother had made another green drink that totally cleared up her arthritis pain. She gave this to some of her friends, and their arthritis pain disappeared, also. She used unsweetened pineapple juice and a variety of fresh, raw, leafy vegetables, such as kale, collards, young Swiss chard leaves, watercress, green outer cabbage leaves, broccoli leaves, Bibb lettuce, or green lettuce leaves, or any available green leafy vegetables that she could find, as well as green bell pepper sections. Occasionally she would add small amounts of herbs, such as sweet basil, peppermint, sweet fennel, comfrey, parsley, or endive.

But back to Daddy's cancer. The doctor checked Daddy once a month for over a year after his last, cancer-less surgery, and the cancer never came back. Daddy had gone totally vegan on the spot, and was healthy from then on. He lived eight more years.

During those eight years, Daddy didn't take medications of any kind. He only went to the doctor for routine check-ups, except when his aorta ruptured, and when he had a fall that resulted in a cracked spine. One doctor that he went to for a check-up didn't believe that, at his age, he wasn't taking any medications, and didn't have a regular primary care doctor. After finding this out, she threw her hands in the air, in front of Daddy, and looked at me and said, "Well, then, there's nothing that I can do; he obviously doesn't need me." She didn't know anything she could recommend without recommending drugs that he wouldn't take anyway.

God promises, "If thou wilt diligently hearken to the voice of the Lord thy God, and wilt do that which is right in his sight, and wilt give ear to his commandments, and keep all His statutes, I will put none of these diseases upon thee ... for I am the Lord that healeth thee" (Exod. 15:26).

Daddy loved life and helping people. Everywhere Daddy lived, he always got involved helping people in the community. Here's an example In one community in Tennessee where Daddy and my stepmother, Joan, had lived, not one person knew anything about what ALL Daddy had been doing until they moved away from the community. Daddy had gone around telling all his community friends good-bye and took some little gift to each of them in the form of a book, magazine, or pamphlet of something encouraging to help them. They all appreciated the gift, but were sad that he was leaving. Some even cried because they didn't want him to go.

A couple of weeks after Daddy and Joan left, the local Seventh-day Adventist Church in that area started getting phone calls like:

"Amos always took out my trash on Tuesdays, because I'm handicapped and can't carry it. Can you please send someone else to take it out for me?"

Another caller said, "Can you send someone every morning to bring my newspaper from the driveway to my porch? I'm in a wheelchair and can't get down the steps."

Another caller asked: "Do you have anyone that can unstop my kitchen sink? Amos always did that."

Someone else shared, "My lawn mower has quit again. Amos always fixed it. Can you send someone else to help me?"

Another asked, "Do you have someone that can pick up my grandchildren from school next Thursday? Amos always picked them up when my daughter has to work and can't go get them."

> *Daddy said to me later, "Even in death, we can be witnesses for God"*

Yet another: "Is there someone there that can change this light bulb for me? I broke my leg and can't climb the ladder. Amos always came by once a week and would do these things for me."

There were many more callers. Daddy had made many friends, including the county government officials. He and they met often at the local "greasy spoon," as Daddy called the restaurant, to talk about everything over lunch.

One day, the county coroner and Daddy were talking, and he found out that Daddy was a Seventh-day Adventist, and he said, "I just love you Seventh-day Adventists that don't eat meat. After you die, yours are the easiest blood vessels to embalm. Your blood vessels are soft and pliable and easy to get the fluid through. People that eat meat have hard, brittle blood vessels that crack and break, and they are so difficult to embalm."

Daddy said to me later, "Even in death, we can be witnesses for God."

Daddy (and Mother, too, when she was living) took Jesus' words and the great commission to heart wherever they lived: "Thou shalt love thy neighbour as thyself" (Matt. 19:19, Mark 12:31) and "Go ye into all the world" (Mark 16:15).

Beetle Load

One morning I was getting ready to brush my teeth at the bathroom sink, when my eye caught a movement to the right on the side of the sink. I looked over to see what it was, and lo, there was a small black ant carrying a huge, dead, black beetle that was at least ten times as big as he. The ant brought its heavy load up to the top of the sink and ran across to the top of the basin.

Then, as if I wasn't shocked enough, that hard-working, heavy laden ant leaned out over the basin. He was standing on and holding onto the sink with his back feet, and leaning out, holding the beetle with his two front legs. He was literally holding the big beetle out over the abyss of the sink. This position let our industrious ant see all over this big sink, to decide which was the best direction to carry his burden.

After some time, Mr. Ant came to the conclusion that he had best be going around the big hole—not down through it and back up. Hence, he proceeded around the rim of that big hole (the sink). When he and his burden were safely on the other side, Mr. Ant proceeded down the other side and took home his day's earning to his family for their supper.

In taking this supper home to his family, not one time did I see Mr. Ant stop to rest because he was tired. Nor did I hear him complain and gripe about the job he was given! He seemed to take his duty seriously and stuck with it until it was done.

God said through Solomon, the wisest man who ever lived, "Go to the ant, thou sluggard; consider her ways, and be wise" (Prov. 6:6).

Now we can see why!

Only One Hand

Dog-sitting for my daughter was quite a change in my life, having no pets of my own at that time. He only came to visit for one week, but we got off to a horrendous start. Gus is a medium-sized, black retriever that enjoys life to the fullest. He thinks everybody is his friend, therefore, everything should be fun and usually it is.

Early on our first morning together, Gus wanted to take me for a walk. With his nylon leash in my hand, I opened the back door, and ZOOM! Out the door he dashed after my neighbor's cat, who was dropping by for a visit. The zip speed of the leash immediately took the skin off of two of my fingers and part of the palm of my right hand. The pain was unbearable, I thought.

A few days later a pipe came apart somewhere in the water system between my house and the neighbor's house. So, besides dealing with the bandages on my right hand, now my left hand had to pour bottled water to wash dishes, plus cook and take care of all the regular stuff.

Of course, during that very same week, extra company showed up for dinner. Both house phone and cell phone rang double the usual, the stray neighborhood cats and dogs were all around for me to feed, and forty-eleven other things happened that needed more than my one hand could handle. I'm embarrassed to say, I lost it! I was grumpy plus!

As I dropped to my knees to pray beside my bed that night, I told God all about it, including feeling sorry for myself because my bandaged hand hurt SO BAD!

Then God impressed me that my hand didn't have a nail in it. My hand was only skinned up. And it was ONLY ONE HAND—not both hands. I was all out of sorts because of all that had happened TO ME, POOR LITTLE ME. I wasn't even thinking of anyone else that I had hurt verbally that day because of my grumpiness, much less loving them enough to suffer and die for them. I now felt so horribly selfish.

Jesus' hands hurt—both of them—and His feet, and more. But He wasn't complaining. He wasn't even thinking of Himself at all! He was suffering and dying for all those people around Him and all of us down through the ages. He was suffering for me, for you. All I could see in my mind that night there on my knees was His hand with the hole and the blood. For a brief moment, I felt a sick pain in my chest.

I poured out to Him how sorry I was for thinking only of myself; and I pray every day that I will overcome sin, so that His death for me will not have been in vain. Suddenly, my hand didn't hurt so bad·! 1 hope and pray that I will always remember those hands with the nail holes in them, and never think of myself again.

"For God so loved the world, that he gave his only begotten Son, that whosoever believeth in him should not perish, but have everlasting life" (John 3:16).

The Shoes

The first Sabbath that I wore my summer Sabbath shoes, the heel broke off. When I went into town on the following Wednesday, I took the shoes to the only shoe repair shop in our town. The lady behind the counter said, "The repair man that fixes that type of break is behind three months; they will be ready in three months."

"THREE MONTHS!" I yelled. It was now May. "That would make it August! Summer will be over by then," I wailed. "I won't be able to wear them at all this season! Where else can I take them?"

The lady said that the nearest shoe repair shop that fixes that type of break is in another city, which for us is an hour away.

I couldn't go that far just to repair shoes, so I reluctantly left them, saying, "Well, I can't wear them like they are, and they have to be fixed. So I might as well leave them here."

The next day was Thursday. I prayed for God to help me have some shoes to wear for Sabbath.

Friday, the second day, at 3:00 pm, my phone rang. It was the lady at the shoe repair shop! "Your shoes are ready. You can pick them up."

Totally surprised and very happy, I said, "I thought they wouldn't be ready for three months?"

She said, "I know, I was surprised, too. But the man who repairs them came in yesterday, and forgot and started on the wrong end of the line of shoes. And since yours were the last ones to come in, he started with yours. And then he realized that he had started on the wrong end and went back to the other end of the line of shoes. Yours were the only ones he fixed on that end."

Isn't God *awesome?* He rules the universe. He keeps the stars in place, the planets, sun, and moon in their orbits. He rules all the other worlds. And yet He cares about you and me and all our little idiosyncrasies, even our shoes. He arranged it so that I didn't have to go a single Sabbath without my Sabbath shoes! Don't you love the way God keeps His promises to us?!

"But seek ye first the kingdom of God, and his righteousness; and all these things shall be added unto you" (Matt. 6:33).

All in Two Weeks

On January 31, 2009, at 4:00 a.m., I found my daddy, Amos Crowder, age eighty-nine, lying on the living room floor. I got him as comfortable as possible and called 911. The ambulance took him to the closest hospital. It was thought at first that he had had a heart attack, but the symptoms were not entirely consistent with a heart attack. They transferred him to one of the top heart hospitals in the state. There they discovered that an aneurysm in his aorta had ruptured, and blood was leaking into his chest cavity. When he discovered this, the surgeon rushed into the room where we were and told Daddy, "You can either die in five minutes on this table, or you can die on the operating table, because no one your age ever makes it through open heart surgery, but that is your only hope."

By then, Daddy's skin color was gray and he was so weak that he was only able to whisper. He whispered, "Surgery."

The doctors and nurses rushed around and got ready for surgery. The doctor told me four times, "Your dad won't make it. Not at his age. He's going to die."

Just as they were rushing him to surgery, Daddy's pastor and head elder showed up to anoint him. The doctors and nurses all stopped right there and waited for Daddy to be anointed, which was a miracle in itself, as they wouldn't normally take time in such an emergency. That made all the difference. "Is any sick among you? let him call for the elders of the church and let them pray over him, anointing him with oil in the name of the Lord: And the prayer of faith shall save the sick, and the Lord shall raise him up" (James 5:14, 15).

The doctor told me later that when the aorta ruptures, a person only lives about fifteen minutes. From the time I found Daddy on the floor until they rolled him into surgery was ten and a half hours! God kept him alive!

The last thing the doctor told me before he went into surgery was this: "Plan his funeral, because he's not going to make it. It's a *six-hour* surgery. I'll call you if he dies before that." They wheeled him away at 2:30 p.m.

Three hours later they called me to the consultation room to see the doctor. Fearing the worst, my friend (who had come to be with me during the surgery) and I entered the room. The doctor entered, came straight toward me, and shook my hand, smiling, as he said, "The surgery went well and he made it. I've never had a surgery like that go that fast!"

God not only kept Daddy living for ten-and-a-half hours even though his life blood was draining away, He also brought him safely through open heart surgery! When God works, He does a complete job!

When Daddy got out of surgery, he was the only patient that his nurse had to care for, even though they were short-handed that night. He (the nurse) stayed right by Daddy's side all night, monitoring the twenty-plus tubes and IVs involved. God arranged for Daddy to have his own personal nurse for the crucial first twenty-four hours. This nurse told me to go home and sleep, and gave me his phone extension so I could check up on Daddy. Once during the night, when I called, the nurse said, "This is the most remarkable patient I have ever had! He is so appreciative! Everything I do for him, he whispers 'Thank you.'" Even in his stuporous condition, God used Daddy for a witness. After only about thirty-six hours, Daddy was doing so much better that he was moved from ICU to step-down (a section in the hospital where a patient can still be closely observed before going to a regular room).

> *God not only kept Daddy living for ten-and-a-half hours even though his life blood was draining away, He also brought him safely through open heart surgery! When God works, He does a complete job!*

A couple of days later, I was on the hospital elevator when two surgeons got on. I asked, "Did either of you work last Saturday afternoon?"

They both said "no," and then one excitedly said to the other, "That was when they had that incredible surgery! That man was eighty-nine, and he lived through open-heart surgery! I understand he's doing quite well."

I told them that was my daddy and they were so amazed at how well he was doing. It seemed that the whole hospital was talking about the "miracle man." Throughout that hospital stay, two different nurses told me that they had never known anyone in that age bracket to make it through such extensive heart surgery.

Over the few months prior to this incident, Daddy and I had been handing out little positive, encouraging Christian books, called *Help in Daily Living*, by E. G. White. If the latest order of books had been on time, we would have already given them all out. But God, in His wisdom, helped the book order to come two weeks late. They arrived the day before Daddy went into the hospital. So that gave us a whole box full to pass out at the hospital. Daddy wanted everyone that helped him to have one of the books. God's glory was shown over and over again in all these miraculous happenings.

The main rehabilitation hospital for western North Carolina usually only takes stroke and orthopedic patients. God worked another miracle by getting Daddy accepted there so he could build up his strength. Daddy was discharged from the heart hospital on the fifth day and moved on the sixth day to the rehab hospital. Nine days after his miraculous surgery, he was walking 150 steps and feeding himself! Our God is so-o-o *awesome!*

One evening, while walking through the lobby of the hospital to the exit, my cell phone rang. I stopped short of the outside door to answer and turned away from the noisy exit to talk. This made me face a lobby full of people of whom I was temporarily unaware. I proceeded to answer the questions of the man on the other end of the line. He was a total stranger from another hospital office, seeking some information. I told him I was in the heart hospital and he asked me why. I proceeded to tell him the miracles involved with Daddy's incident. The stranger, too, was impressed with what God had done.

After we hung up, I was replacing my phone in my purse when a lady sitting across the room facing me came over to me and said, "I'm sorry, I didn't mean to be listening to your phone conversation, but could you please tell me more of those miracles?" Her eyes were watering. I listened to her story. Her husband was upstairs, had just had open-heart surgery, and wasn't doing very well. They were not sure if he would live. We talked more about God's miracles, and I gave her an encouraging book. I asked her husband's name and told her that I, too, would pray for him that night.

The next morning, as I came through the front door of the heart hospital, that dear lady was waiting in the lobby with a smile on her face and came straight to me. "Thank you for praying for my husband," she said. "He's better this morning and is going to be able to go home!" Isn't God *awesome?!*

Satan couldn't stand for me to praise God all over the hospital to everyone I saw: doctors, nurses, janitors, cafeteria people, and more. So, after spending less than a week in the hospital with Daddy, I came down with an infection in my lip! My face swelled and turned beet red! I had a high fever and got very sick. After seeing four very concerned and helpful doctors, it was discovered that I had MRSA, a very dangerous and mostly fatal infection. The doctors said it could have killed me instantly, being so close to my brain. After a traumatic surgery to drain the pockets of infection, the MRSA was gone in one week! Again, God intervened! I was told that MRSA never goes away that fast. Again, I say, we serve an *awesome* God!

Yes, friends, God still works miracles today!

The Airplane Delay

God's will, not mine (ours).

I had not seen my son's family, with my four grandchildren, for a whole year and three months. So, naturally, I was excited to finally be flying the two thousand plus miles to spend a few weeks with them. The plane ticket included two stops for plane changes, a trip of nine hours from my home.

After we boarded the second plane at the first stop, we sat there onboard and waiting, and waiting, to finally hear the announcement over the intercom that something was wrong with the plane and to "sit tight" and that it would be fixed "momentarily."

I was sitting by a window. God had arranged that the man next to me should be an airplane mechanic for that very airline. Bob was very tall and broad shouldered, so after he returned from discussing things with the pilot and crew, it took him a few minutes to re-adjust himself in the middle seat.

While he was gone, I prayed, "Lord, how do You want me to witness to such a businesslike man?" I really wanted to lay my head against the wall and sleep while I had the opportunity. This, I thought, would help keep me from being so frustrated after all this delay that I might possibly miss my next connecting flight to my family.

But, as usual, God didn't want me thinking of myself and my situation. He wanted me not to waste one moment when I could be working for Him. So, immediately, as soon as I prayed, "How do you want me to witness?" the health magazines in my carry-on came to my mind!!

While Bob was re-adjusting in his seat, I was pulling out the *Eight Laws of Health* magazine. Thinking I could just hand it to Bob and then take my nap, I gave it to him with a short explanation and turned my head toward the window for my desperately needed sleep.

> *But, as usual, God didn't want me thinking of myself and my situation. He wanted me not to waste one moment when I could be working for Him*

But, no. Again what I wanted could wait. Bob turned out to be one of these people that can read the whole page at a brief glance. Bob opened the first page, immediately commented on its contents, and began asking me questions. The whole health issue popped open, and a great discussion was immediately in progress.

After the second page discussion, I realized that the man in the aisle seat next to Bob was looking over his shoulder at the magazine, too, and taking in every word that was said. I took out another of the same issue of the health magazine and held it out toward him.

"Thank you," he said, as he readily took it and opened it to the same page.

At some time during that exciting conversation, our plane must have taken off from the Chicago gate, because, all of a sudden, we were landing in Denver! Yes, we were late, and I missed my flight in Denver, but what if a soul is saved because of it?

Bob said he was going to start eating healthy, drinking more water, and exercising now to help his blood pressure and the other physical problems his body was starting to have. Thank you, God, for the delay.

But by then, when the ticket agent checked, there were no more flights out that night to my destination of Spokane. I was going to have to spend the night in the airport. But, guess what!? There was a seat on another airline going back to Minneapolis/St. Paul, and then maybe I could get a flight from there to Spokane. So, back-tracking I went.

I arrived at the Minneapolis/St. Paul airport just in time to get one of the last seats on a Spokane-bound flight, right next to—you guessed it—a husband and wife, both wanting to talk and having some horrible problems with health. They, too, were delighted with the new knowledge of God's way of healing that they were obtaining from *Eight Laws of Health*, and they especially loved the "Trust in God" one. They also had small grandchildren and were delighted with all the various children's stories about Jesus that I gave them, which, incidentally, God had reminded me to put in my carry-on as well.

I did finally meet my precious family, and for the two-hour drive home in their van, I had all these new stories to tell of my fifteen-hour (instead of nine-hour) trip out to them, and how, again, God's will is always best.

"Saying, Father, if thou be willing, remove this cup from me: nevertheless not my will, but thine, be done" (Luke 22:42).

Heart Attack

One Sunday afternoon, my daughter, Katy, came from Tennessee to North Carolina to visit. As she came through our front door, I had dinner ready and was just carrying it to the dining room. My Daddy was already waiting at the table. After we finished eating, we sat at the table talking, when suddenly, I got really nauseated. I said to my family, "Oh, I'm so sick," as I got up and went to my bedroom. I sat down on my bed and Katy came running with a bucket.

Just as she got to me, I started sweating profusely. Then the horrible pain hit—at first in my chest, then immediately all over my body. I grabbed my chest and said, "Oh, the pain," and fainted over onto the bed.

Katy, recognizing the symptoms, called 911. They were there, up our mountain, in seven minutes, I was told later. God brought Katy here one hour before my heart attack, or else there would have been no one to call 911, because Daddy was still in the dining room and did not see what was happening.

God brought me to consciousness in time to hear what He wanted me to hear. I was aware briefly of people working with me, and evidently answered their questions about the pain. Then I was unconscious again. I regained consciousness just as a male voice (paramedic) said, "She's having the heart attack right now."

In my shocked mind, though, I couldn't open my eyes, I silently threw it at God. "God, a heart attack? Why a heart attack? Why me? I eat right, I exercise, I drink water, I get sunshine." I went through part of the eight laws of health right there with God, asking why?

God very simply said to me, "Just stand back and watch." Right at that moment when He put that thought into my mind, there was peace. I felt such wonderful peace. It was all okay. If I lived, fine, if I died, fine. It didn't matter anymore. I was in God's hands. I felt so very safe and at total peace from then on.

"For my thoughts are not your thoughts, neither are your ways my ways, saith the Lord" (Isa. 55:8).

Heart Attack | 69

The next time I regained consciousness, I was in the ambulance. There was a large man climbing into the back of the ambulance, panting as he said, "Rita, I'm Mike, and I'll be taking care of you." Just then a woman passed the window shouting, "I'll start the motor."

That broke the tension in my mind, thinking of it as funny. A man that is puffing and sounds like he's the one going to have a heart attack is taking care of me! And there's a woman driving the ambulance! Even though it seemed funny to me, I was very thankful for her driving. But then I was out again. I woke up three times in the ambulance. All three times Mike was yelling to the driver, "Hold the siren. I can't get her blood pressure, again." Later, they told me I almost died three times in the ambulance.

The next time God brought me to consciousness, they were pulling me on the stretcher out of the back of the ambulance. Mike was holding the door for them. As I went by him, I looked up and he was crying. He said, "Rita, I'll be praying for you." I never saw him before or since, but that meant so very much to me. I will always remember Mike, who took such good care of me in the ambulance.

The next time I came around, I was in a bed in a small room with a nurse doing something. I glanced through the open door, and here came my precious daughter pushing my beloved Daddy in a wheelchair to see me. It was so good to see them. We spoke a few happy words; I remember their encouraging smiles. Then I was out again.

The next time I came to consciousness, I was lying in a very cold, large room with lots of lights, very, very bright, and many people in uniforms rushing all around, all talking to me, saying, "I'm so-and-so, and I'm going to do such-and-such." They all seemed to be very nice, but I couldn't comprehend any of it. I remember thinking, "Well, just do it!"

Right then, a man dressed in a very nice suit walked up to the foot of my stretcher. I learned later that he was the surgeon. I heard the nurse that was standing there say to him, "This one is totally vegan." The surgeon said, "Oh, good, then we won't have to worry about her recovery." I said in my mind to God, "Okay, God, I get it. Just do whatever you want to do with me." Then I was unconscious again; only this time, while I was asleep, they did open heart surgery, including a heart catheterization and quadruple bypass.

I regained consciousness in the recovery room in the wee hours of the next morning. There were two nurses attending me in the dimly-lit room. Suddenly, in bounded a third nurse, who jumped up on a desk across the room and sat Indian-style on the desk. She said, "I've been studying into this vegan thing a lot, and there REALLY IS something to it."

Both of my nurses turned around away from me, looking at her, and said, "Oh, really?" Then they started asking her questions about the vegan lifestyle. She answered a few of their questions, but then could not answer any more. At that moment, God rallied me totally awake. I raised up on my elbow, turning toward all three of them, and God, through me, answered all their questions.

One nurse said, "That's great! I want to do that." The next one said, "I want to eat like that, too."

The third one said, "Me, too."

The nurse on the desk got down and went out of the room. The other two were turning back toward me as I lay back down and went totally back to sleep.

Later that morning, I woke up again. This time I was in a single room and the sun was shining in the window—a bright, beautiful day. My precious daughter, Katy, who I found out later had been there all night, was sitting next to me, and got up and came toward me as I opened my eyes. The door to my room was open and out in the hall people were walking by, talking.

Every once in a while, someone in the hall would say, "This is where that vegan is." Or, "That vegan is in this room." Now and then a head would pop in around the corner of the door, look at me, and then go back out and would say to the other person, "Oh, that one," like I was some kind of a novelty.

Then, as some felt a little braver, one would come all the way into my room and ask questions that God helped Katy and me both to answer. Evidently, word about God's vegan diet had already circulated through the whole heart tower, telling about how well this vegan was doing, and how fast she was getting well after having almost died just a few hours before.

I still didn't totally understand what was happening until the morning of the fourth day after my heart attack. My surgeon walked into my hospital room and said, "Girl, the rest of your body is just fine, your blood work was excellent through the whole thing, your lifestyle has given you a healthy body; just go home and get well. You don't need to be in here."

Wow! I was alive after a major heart attack and heart catheterization and quadruple bypass, and I could go home on the fourth day! Of course, I had to rest and not do a whole lot at first. But I was home with my family and could see my friends.

God was definitely in this! He also arranged for my daughter Katy to be able to stay for a few weeks to help us at home. She took over my rehab, and scheduled visitors to spread their visits apart. She unselfishly gave up her new job to which she was transferring so she could take care of her grandpa and me. Later, God provided another really good job in southern California for her in its place.

My first follow-up visit to my cardiologist (never had had one before) told the rest of the story.

He told me the medical reason why I had the heart attack to begin with. I already knew at this point that God had used my heart attack for His honor and glory, to spread the knowledge of His healthy lifestyle to many other people. And now, this doctor explained that I had had four blockages. Two were 90% blocked and two were 100% blocked. He said the blockages were very old. He said, "I will guess the blockages were twelve to fifteen years old."

Then he asked me, "When did you started eating vegan?"

I answered, "Thirteen years ago."

Then the cardiologist said, "Well, that's it. If you had not started eating vegan when you did, you would have died then. Your heart has been building its own bypass!" He held up his hand with his thumb and forefinger about one-quarter-inch apart and said, "Your bypass was this much from being finished; and if you had been getting enough sleep it would have finished and you would NOT have had the heart attack."

> *God had used my heart attack for His honor and glory, to spread the knowledge of His healthy lifestyle to many other people*

The doctor had learned from my daughter that in helping and taking care of other people, I was up day and night and not getting a whole night's sleep. For many years, I had the mentality that I could sleep when I got old, because I was too busy now. I didn't realize that NOT getting enough sleep will make you old.

The doctor then said to me, "Girl, your vegan lifestyle saved your life." He said that Katy's fast response calling 911, and my healthy lifestyle, saved me, as I would never have even made it to the hospital.

Maybe this is a good time to mention GOD'S PLAN (From https://1ref.us/th, accessed Sept. 19, 2019):

G = Godly Trust

O = Open Air

D = Daily Exercise

S = Sunshine

P = Plenty of Rest

L = Lots of Water

A = Always Temperate

N = Nutrition

These are the eight laws of health mentioned earlier to stay healthy. I was doing all of them except the "**P**" (Plenty of Rest). Now I know that of the eight laws, each one is just as important as the others. Again, God was there teaching many people, including me.

"Thank You, Lord!"

"Wait on the Lord; be of good courage, and he shall strengthen thine heart; wait, I say, on the Lord" (Ps. 27:14).

The Wad

While my daughter, Katy, lived in Southern California, Daddy and I had the privilege of visiting her for a few months. While there, I was able to join her and her dog, Gus (my fun-loving, dog-sitting buddy), for their evening walks. One evening, our walk was later than usual. We were walking along the public sidewalks, talking and laughing, when, about twenty feet to the side of us, by a fence, we saw something round and black in the dusk—something round and black and moving. To our horror, whatever it was was moving straight toward us and gaining speed.

Katy reeled in Gus, who also now saw the black round "wad" and wanted to get to it. Just about that time, Katy realized what it was, and said, "It's a SKUNK!"

It turns out, that community was loaded with skunks. It seems that skunks like people. So here comes this round, black wad, as Katy named it, right toward us! By now it was dark, but we could see the wad of skunks. As it got closer, we saw that actually there was a father, mother, and three babies. Five! And yet they were all together in a wad! They were in such agreement, in such unity, in such accord, that it truly looked like one fat skunk! They stayed right together, walking and running together, not one going off by themselves, or straggling behind the others ... not one of them wandering off. There was no dissension of any kind.

We rushed a distance away and stopped to watch. They were waiting to cross the busy three lane street. So many fast cars were going by! The little skunk family stopped on the curb and, seeing no break in the traffic, rushed back ten feet or so toward the fence, moving and watching all the time—never still, but always together in their wad. Every little bit they would go back to the curb to check the traffic.

Finally, there were no cars. The cute little wad then split up. The dad ran across the street first, to show them how, then the mother and the babies followed, running in single file. The curb on the other side of the street was about a foot higher than the side they were coming from because of the downward slope of the road. The dad jumped up over the curb and ran across the side walk to the trees and waited. The mother leaped up over the curb, too, and joined the dad.

The first baby made the leap okay, and joined its parents; the second baby, too, and joined its family. The third baby, smaller than the others, leaped and missed, leaped and missed, leaped and then finally succeeded in joining his family, and, together again in their wad, they disappeared up the hill through the trees.

Watching God's little creatures operate in such unity and togetherness was VERY impressive. At times they were so cooperative they even moved as one. Maybe we humans can learn something from them.

Also, they seemed very patient, waiting for the right time to cross the street. Even the children did not seem to be complaining about the delay. They continued to stay with, and obey, their parents.

"In your patience possess ye your souls" (Luke 21:19).

Trenton Luke

I had been studying in Psalms and had discovered many of God's promises. One especially caught my eye—Psalm 41:1, 2, and 3. So the very next month, which was August, when my thirteen-year-old grandson, Trenton, was diagnosed with a rare leukemia, and we were all heartbroken, I decided to claim that new found promise while I was praying in Trenton's behalf.

"The LORD will deliver him in time of trouble [in his case leukemia]. the LORD will preserve [protect] him, and keep him alive; and he shall be blessed upon the earth: and thou wilt not deliver him unto the will of his enemies [Satan causing leukemia]. The LORD will strengthen him upon the bed of languishing: thou wilt make all his bed in his sickness."

I was able to visit Trenton and his family in Idaho some during his treatments and hospitalization. The last time I saw Trenton in the hospital, before returning to my home in North Carolina, I hugged and kissed him. As I was going out the door of his room, I said, "Trenton, keep looking up."

Laughingly, he said, "Grandma, that's the only way I CAN look, lying here in bed."

Trenton and I talked many times on the telephone after that. Through the months, I kept praying for my precious grandson, and claiming Psalm 41. In May, before Trenton's fourteenth birthday, I called to talk to him. He said, "Everybody around here is crying, and thinks I'm dying. Grandma, do you think I'm going to die, too?"

Swallowing the lump in my throat, I said, "No, Trenton, I called to see what you want for your birthday."

Happily, he said, "Oh, good, I'm glad," and started talking about his birthday.

Two weeks after his fourteenth birthday, I was sitting in my living room, in North Carolina, visiting with guests, when Mitchell and Evelyn (Trenton's other grandparents) came walking in the front door. Evelyn was carrying a box of tissues. I knew already what that meant. As our eyes met, I asked, "He died?"

She nodded. We embraced each other as we both burst into tears. Mitchell and Evelyn stayed with me for a while that evening, for encouragement, then went home to try to get some sleep. I had claimed that promise in Psalm 41, but Trenton died anyway. Still crying, I took my Bible to my room, and opened it to that promise, knelt down beside my bed, facing the window, and placed the open Bible on the bed in front of me.

Yelling at God between my sobs, I pounded on that Bible verse and screamed, "GOD, THIS DOESN'T WORK! THIS DOESN'T WORK!" I was sobbing uncontrollably by now.

The moon that had just passed my window moments before and had gone out of sight, miraculously moved back and shone very brightly straight into my face, blinding me enough to stop my yelling and quiet me down. After I was quieted, God gently impressed me, saying, "I'm still here." After a pause, "Are you going to TRUST ME?"

Quieting down, I said "yes." Then, still sobbing, "I still trust You, but I don't understand."

Very calmly, God said, "Romans 9:6."

So, I turned in my Bible to that verse, and read, "Not as though the word of God hath taken none effect [has failed]. For they are not all Israel, which are of Israel:"

So it was not that God's Word had failed. He showed me that because not everybody knows God's love like I do, that He is going to use that young boy's death for His own honor and glory.

God showed me that the promises that I had claimed WILL be kept in God's timing, not mine.

The first thing to happen after Trenton's death that I witnessed was the memorial service. The church was packed. A lot of the people were teenagers, asking the same question, "WHY?"

The memorial service was very upbeat. Katy and I sang, "What a Day That Will Be." And the poems, songs, sermon—every aspect of it—was about Jesus' coming again (John 14:1–3), waking Trenton up (1 Thess. 4:16–18), and all of us going to heaven together. There were also beautiful Bible promises.

After the service, various people of different beliefs came up to family members and said things like: "I didn't know the Bible said that. I'm going home and study my Bible more." God was already using this boy's death to bring people to Jesus and help them learn more about Him.

In the next witness that I know of, Trenton's family had started a website in his memory, teaching the health message—and much more—

around the world. His name means "Swift Runner" so the website is swiftrunnerministries.com (https://1ref.us/ti, accessed Sept. 9, 2019) The last I knew, the website was in over 200 countries! God is spreading the gospel all over the world in many ways, including using this precious boy's death. It is so *awesome* how God is working. Everything God does is for our ultimate good.

In looking back, I can see how Trenton, his daddy, Dallas, and all of his family, were used as witnesses for God in the hospital, to the doctors, nurses, and other staff. When I visited in the hospital, different nurses and staff told me:

"We have never had a patient like Trenton before!"

"Trenton and his family are so close to each other!"

"Trenton and his family are so close to God!"

"Trenton really encourages me!"

God allowed Trenton to spend his last five months at home with his mother and daddy and his siblings. Also, God helped him to feel well enough to play with his sisters and brother, go camping, canoeing, biking, and work on his hobbies of taking pictures and "computering." Trenton was the computer genius behind his family's website, Biblepicturepathways.com (https://1ref.us/th, accessed Sept. 19, 2019).

God was so merciful to Trenton and to his family to allow us to have this energetic, ingenious, and compassionate son, brother, nephew, and grandson for fourteen wonderful years.

Trenton is still facing up buried on his mountain, at the edge of his woods, beside his favorite climbing tree, overlooking the beautiful valley that he loved to photograph, waiting for his Saviour, Jesus Christ, to come and call him up from his grave.

"Blessed are the dead which die in the Lord from henceforth: Yea, saith the Spirit, that they may rest from their labours; and their works do follow them" (Rev. 14:13).

Bus "Wreck"

I had a CDL (Commercial Driver License) for many years. During that time I drove my husband's eighteen-wheeler truck several times when the children and I were with him on trips and he would get too sleepy to drive but needed to keep going. But mostly I drove the school bus for almost twelve of those years. I loved every minute of it. The children on the bus were so enjoyable.

One summer a local church asked me to drive their bus to take their F.L.A.G. Camp (Fun Learning About God) children to the Leila Patterson Center in Fletcher, North Carolina, for a swimming session.

It has always been a habit of mine to have prayer with the children before we take off on any activity trip. So, after prayer, we took off to go the six miles to the center that has exercise workout rooms, gymnasium, and swimming pools, among other things.

As we cautiously crossed the railroad tracks, I was picking back up to the allotted speed, already going about thirty-five mph, when suddenly around the curve from the other direction came a light-colored pickup truck driving very erratically. It was all over the road—back and forth across both lanes. It was headed straight toward us!

I knew that there was no shoulder on that narrow, two-lane road. The edge of the pavement dropped straight down into a two-and-a-half to three-foot ditch. So, in the few seconds I had to decide how to protect that bus load of children, I prayed a quick, frantic prayer and tried to get over as far as I could to the road's edge without dropping the right wheel off of the pavement. Fearing the truck was going to hit us, I went too far, and the front bus wheel dropped off the road, taking the whole bus load of precious passengers to the ditch, right between two power poles, missing both of them.

The bus miraculously went into slow motion and laid gently over on its side on the ground. At the speed we had been going, the impact of going into that rough, bumpy ditch should have thrown the children, teachers, and me into the windows and sides of the bus (there were no seat belts on the bus); but, miraculously, everyone was still in their seats after the impact!

A little six-year-old girl two seats back behind me said after the impact, "That seemed like angels were laying us down very gently!"

After we hit the ground, everyone was sitting sideways, but everyone was stone silent at the shock of still being alive and not hurt. In the silence—so strong everyone could hear to the back of the bus—I said, "Is everybody okay?"

"Yes," came back repeatedly, over and over from children and teachers.

A little six-year-old girl two seats back behind me said after the impact, "That seemed like angels were laying us down very gently!"

It truly did. The whole thing happened so fast, but it truly did feel like the bus was being held and **gently** being laid over instead of banging and crashing and throwing everyone around like it would normally do at that speed while it was falling over on its side.

On our side of the road was a field of tall corn stalks. God immediately put into my mind that there was a mowed field straight across the street from us with a building, which turned out to be a doctor's office.

I said, kindly, but sternly, to the three teachers on board, "Open that back door, and help the children out one by one and across the street to that field, away from the traffic." (Obviously, we could not use the front door, since it was lying against the ground.)

As the teachers were assisting the children at the back of the bus, a policeman in his patrol car pulled up to the front of the bus to my window, and looking up and over at me from his car window, asked, "Is anyone hurt?"

I answered, "No, sir."

He said, "What happened?"

Just as he asked that, an excited woman from the second car behind us (all the traffic behind us had totally stopped to let the children get across the road) came running up, yelling, "I saw the whole thing! I saw the whole thing! That pickup truck was going to hit them. This driver [pointing at me] couldn't do anything else! She was trying to avoid a head-on collision with that truck!"

The policeman looked at me and said, "Is that what happened?"

I said, "Yes, sir."

He and I both thanked the lady, and she went back to her car.

He looked at me and put his ticket book away as he said, "I'm not even going to record this," and drove away.

Here was the bus lying on its side on the ground. All forty-eight passengers, children ages six to twelve, three teachers, and the driver, totally unharmed—not even so much as a bumped head on the windows, and not even a scratch on any of us! This all was a miracle!

After the policeman left, I checked all through the bus and then joined the children over in the field. The doctor's office was allowing everyone to use their restroom facilities and get drinks from their drinking fountain.

A reporter from a western North Carolina TV station was there talking to different ones of us to see what had happened and how we all were doing, so then we were all on the 6:00 evening news that night. Everyone could see the whole thing was a total miracle. None of us needed to go to the emergency room nor see a doctor.

But wait! There's more to this miracle! A big wrecker came, pulled the bus upright, and then pulled it all the way out of the ditch. A couple of men who had stopped to help knocked away the big dirt clods that had collected on the ground side of the bus. There wasn't even one single slight dent or scratched place on the bus. The side door opened just fine. I got in and started the engine, and it worked as well.

The teachers brought the children over, and all filed through the working door into our newly up-righted bus. I closed the door and we happily went on our way to our swimming destination.

The light-colored pickup truck had kept going, probably not even realizing what he had caused. Hopefully, he, too, was thankful there had not been a collision. Every time I thank God for protecting our bus and all its passengers, I pray that that man sees God in his life, too—and is grateful.

My Daddy

Through the years, I had always prayed for my loving parents, Amos and Kate Crowder. So, when my daddy at age eighty-six came to live with me, I started praying that he would have some personal recognition for the fact that he served in World War II fighting for our freedom. The stories he had told me of his experiences were horrendous, and although I and other family members had thanked him many times for his service, I wanted him to know that he was dearly loved and appreciated.

I called a couple of radio and TV stations to see about going that route, but was always told, "There's so-o-o many World War II veterans, and we already did a story on that last year."

So I kept praying. Of course, Daddy didn't know I was thinking that way. He would have never wanted any recognition. I have never known any World War II veteran to be bragging or boastful about their experiences in the war. In fact, because of all the blood and death, they usually won't talk about it. Bringing back the memories makes them cry. They deserve our recognition, though, because without them our country wouldn't be what it is today.

Soon after I started praying for him to be recognized for his service in some way, a man said to me, "Why don't you take your dad to the Veteran's Administration Hospital?" I didn't even know that I could do that, and up until this point, he had been seeing civilian doctors.

I took him to the VA hospital in Asheville, NC, and they sweetly took over his care. They tested him thoroughly and discovered he was 100% disabled as a direct result of his military service. So, from then on, his nurse practitioner, therapists, social worker, dietician, nurse assistants, and anyone he needed or wanted, came to our house to care for his needs. They "bent over backwards" for this World War II veteran. As soon as each member of the staff at the VA Hospital found out he was a World War II veteran, the men saluted him and the women saluted him and kissed his cheek or forehead, and everyone thanked him for his service, every time they saw him.

One day, while we were at the VA, news people were there. A cameraman stopped us in the hall and took pictures and interviewed Daddy. The next morning, Daddy's picture was in the newspaper with his World War II story about how he had served with General George Patton. From then on, every time we went there, Daddy was honored, along with other World War II veterans. He loved going to that VA Hospital for his checkups.

Even seventy years after the war, Daddy still had nightmares of the men around him getting shot down and dying. Even with his daytime naps, he would wake up crying. I would say, "Daddy, why are you crying?"

He would say, "All the men around me were getting shot down." Then through his tears, he would point up and say, "He [meaning God] kept me alive."

Wouldn't those terrible dreams be hard to live with all your life?!

I remembered, when my children were small and had bad dreams at night, that we would pray and ask God to take away their bad dreams, and He did. So one day when I found Daddy crying after he woke up from a nap, I said, "Daddy, let's pray that you won't have any more bad dreams." So, we prayed, and God took them away; Daddy didn't have any more nightmares after that.

> *"All the men around me were getting shot down." Then through his tears, he would point up and say, "He [meaning God] kept me alive"*

Then, one Sunday when he was ninety-four, while we were at the dining room table eating, Daddy got choked on some food. I got the coughing stopped and thought he was okay. But for some reason, he became weak. On Tuesday, I called the VA nurse practitioner, who came out and checked him. She said he needed to go to the hospital. I took him to the VA Hospital, the doctor X-rayed him, and said there was food in Daddy's lungs and it had developed into pneumonia. There was nothing they could do at his age.

I took Daddy home and kept him comfortable. I still had a hospital bed from when I had taken care of patients, so I could adjust it up to a sitting position, and down to a lying down position, to help him be more comfortable. I faced it toward his picture window so he could watch the birds and squirrels at his bird feeder outside the window. Every day he was a little weaker, and I prayed with him several times a day. In answer to our prayers, God kept him from any pain.

Then, on Sabbath afternoon, Dr. Kim and fourteen precious members of our church came to our house, gathered around Daddy's bed, and lined the living room adjoining Daddy's room. They talked to him, prayed with him, and sang old hymns to Daddy for two hours. I saw Daddy's lips moving as he weakly sang along. They sang all his favorites and many more. Some of them were: "Oh, Shepherd Divine," "How Great Thou Art," and "The Old Rugged Cross." He loved it.

When they left, I asked Daddy if he was in any pain and he answered, "No."

I said, "I love you, Daddy."

He said, "I love you, too."

One hour after the singers left, Daddy took his last breath. I was there by his side.

God did it again! Like He did for my mother [her story is in book one], He answered all my prayers, this time for my Daddy. He gave Daddy personal honor for his military service for our country. He helped Daddy not to suffer from the cause of his death, and he helped me to be beside Daddy when he died.

And, as always, God did something extra. He allowed Daddy to die with those beautiful hymns on his mind, feeling happy and content in Jesus and in the hope of the resurrection. What a comfort!

"For the Lord himself shall descend from heaven with a shout, with the voice of the archangel, and with the trump of God: and the dead in Christ shall rise first: Then we which are alive and remain shall be caught up together with them in the clouds, to meet the Lord in the air: and so shall we ever be with the Lord. Wherefore comfort one another with these words" (1 Thess. 4:16–18).

The Old Rugged Cross

1. On a hill far away stood an old rugged cross,
the emblem of suffering and shame;
and I love that old cross where the dearest and best
for a world of lost sinners was slain.

2. O that old rugged cross, so despised by the world,
has a wondrous attraction for me:
for the dear Lamb of God left his glory above
to bear it to dark Calvary.

3. In that old rugged cross, stained with blood so divine,
a wondrous beauty I see,
for 'twas on that old cross Jesus suffered and died,
to pardon and sanctify me.

4. To that old rugged cross I will ever be true,
its shame and reproach gladly bear;
then he'll call me some day to my home far away,
where his glory forever I'll share.

Text: George Bennard, 1913
Tune: George Bennard, 1913

Irregular
THE OLD RUGGED CROSS
www.hymnary.org/text/on_a_hill_far_away_stood_an_old_rugged

This hymn is in the public domain. You may freely use this score for personal and congregational worship. If you reproduce the score, please credit Hymnary.org as the source.

Coral Cliffs Calamity

My friend, Anita, and I had joined some others, including my daughter Katy, her dog Gus, and their friends on a hike around some coral cliffs beside the ocean on the Island of Guam. The tide was out, so no waves were coming up on the cliffs. After about an hour of hiking, Anita and I had fallen way behind the group and decided to turn around and start back. But before heading back, we felt impressed to pray for the others, as we saw them disappearing around the distant coral cliff. At the end of my prayer, out of my mouth came, "And especially be with Katy and keep her safe," not realizing then why the extra prayer for her.

The hikers came to a deep crevasse in the coral, about four feet across. One by one, they were jumping across the crevasse. Katy had turned Gus loose, and he had already jumped across. Katy had hung the leash around her neck to carry it. When it was Katy's turn, she positioned her feet and was just getting ready to jump, when, suddenly, from out of nowhere, a huge wave came crashing up, totally picked Katy up, and sucked her down into the crevasse. The other hikers panicked around the crevasse as they looked down the seven or eight feet to where the water had sunk, and there was no Katy! She had been sucked down even deeper!

Somehow, as she went further beneath the surface, she miraculously stayed in the middle of the open space. While under the water, washing up and down with the waves, at any moment the strong waves could dash her sharply against the jagged coral surrounding her, breaking her bones, and/or hitting her head and knocking her unconscious—or worse. But they didn't! She tried to swim upward toward the light above her, but the strong suction wouldn't let her, and kept her submerged. While she was still under the water, God spoke to Katy, "Hold your arms straight up." Katy immediately obeyed. Then Josh saw one of her hands, squatted down, reached as far as he could, grabbed her hand, and started to pull. But the next wave broke his grasp, sending Katy deeper. Then Pastor Ron rushed up, took hold of Josh, to brace both of them from being sucked in, too.

Together they squatted down, grabbed Katy's two hands with their two free hands and started to pull. Then Ben got down, and when Katy washed up further with their pull, Ben grabbed her legs, and together they broke the suction, and they all pulled Katy to safety. Josh's cell phone, Gus' leash, and Katy's sunglasses were all sucked into the ocean.

The rest of the hikers had been praying frantically together, and God answered their prayers. He used the three men to save her life.

We found out later that that hole is called "The Devil's Hole" because thirty people had already lost their lives there.

Katy said later that she never touched the bottom. It was open on the side out toward the ocean. There was no human way of escaping that watery grave by herself. Our God is an *awesome* God! Praise God for His intervention and protection!

"When thou passest through the waters, I will be with thee" (Isa. 43:2).

Power of Prayer Protection

It was a sunny, cold Sabbath day in northern Idaho. My son, Dallas, with his wife and children, headed out from their home in the mountains to go to church. Thankfully, it is their practice to always have prayer and ask God's blessings and protection when they leave home. And of course, Grandma and others pray for them daily and nightly.

Driving slowly because of the snow and ice, the family had reached the bottom of their mountain, still with a straight stretch of road and a railroad crossing to go. Dallas continued to drive slowly to get to the main highway. Just as their SUV started down the slope toward the railroad tracks, Dallas realized the slope was totally covered with ice. The SUV started sliding immediately. Then it turned sideways, parallel with the railroad tracks, and slid faster.

The engineer of the oncoming train saw the car sliding toward the tracks and laid on his horn, but he could do nothing else. Dallas could do nothing else, either, but pray. They were headed straight for a collision with the train.

Then suddenly, right in the middle of the ice, the SUV stopped, just short of the tracks, as the train zoomed by. God and His angels stopped that SUV! No other way would it have stopped on that slope, with more ice to go, without God's intervention! The whole family would have been killed. But God is so *awesome!* Praise God for His intervention and protection!

This was exactly six months to the weekend after Katy almost drowned half-way around the world in Guam. I would have lost my whole family in six months time, had it not been for God's intervention in both situations, saving all their lives!

"Because he hath set his love upon me, therefore will I deliver him: I will set him on high, because he hath known my name. He shall call upon me, and I will answer him: *I will be with him in trouble; I will deliver him, and honour him*" (Ps. 91:14, 15; emphasis added).

Interview with Dr. Steve Im
—Ultimate Cancer Cure

RITA : Thank you, Dr. Im, for taking time to tell us these valuable truths for healing! How many people have you treated for cancer?

DR. IM : Over a thousand people have been healed from cancer at my clinic.

RITA : How do you do it?

DR. IM : God is the true Healer. When we do what He says, HE heals.

RITA : Please explain.

DR. IM : Philippians 3:20, 21 tells us, "For our conversation is in heaven; from whence also we look for the Saviour, the Lord Jesus Christ: Who shall change our vile body, that it may be fashioned like unto his glorious body, according to the working whereby he is able even to subdue all things unto himself." This tells us that our conversation needs to be in heaven. Then our Lord Jesus Christ will change our vile bodies and fashion them to be like His glorious body, according to how He is able to conquer all things unto Himself.

RITA : What does it mean, "our conversation needs to be in heaven?"

DR. IM : Speak only uplifting words to other people, nothing negative or discouraging.

RITA : Oh, I see! Be positive at all times.

DR. IM : Yes! Then in 1 Corinthians 6:19, 20 we are told: "What? know ye not that your body is the temple of the Holy Ghost which is in you, which ye have of God, and ye are not your own? For ye are bought with a price: therefore glorify God in your body, and in your spirit, which are God's." This tells us that we belong to Jesus. We are born here on this earth. Jesus made us; He created us perfect and to be well, not sick.

But we sinned.

Sin is the transgression of God's law. Sin is the opposite of God. Sin destroys. Romans 6:23 reminds us: "For the wages of sin is death; but the gift of God is eternal life through Jesus Christ our Lord."

RITA : Yes, that's true.

DR. IM : So Jesus died for our sins that He had no part in, and bought us (our bodies) back to Him. So, now we belong to Jesus twice. So we should live HIS life instead of our life. My body is God's body, so I represent Him. We are citizens of heaven so we live Jesus' life, not our life.

RITA : Oh wow! I never thought of that before!

DR. IM : When we are sick we are living our life instead of His. If I speak and think my way, then I will be sick, because I live my way and not His way. My body was bought by Jesus. My Creator died for me. He bought me back with His life.

RITA : Yes—that's beautiful! I love it!

DR. IM : The whole universe belongs to God, but Satan rebelled. If I follow my way, then I belong to Satan.

Galatians 2:20 says, "I am crucified with Christ: nevertheless I live; yet not I, but Christ liveth in me: and the life which I now live in the flesh I live by the faith of the Son of God, who loved me, and gave himself for me."

This tells us that Jesus will live in me, and in you. Keeping His commandments is obeying His way. Unkindness, complaining, and anger shut Jesus out from dwelling in me.

"Angels flee from the dwelling where words of discord are exchanged, where gratitude is almost a stranger to the heart, and censure leaps like black balls to the lips, spotting the garments, defiling the Christian character" (White, *Testimonies for the Church,* vol. 1, 695.2).

When I live God's way, I cannot get sick. Anger produces bad hormones; it produces norepinephrine, a stress hormone which raises blood pressure and can cause memory loss.

Anger causes acid blood; anger causes lack of oxygen which causes headaches; lack of exercise also causes lack of oxygen. Lack of oxygen causes brain cells to be damaged so they can't function properly. Then you cannot think right, and negative thoughts occur, causing depression and memory loss.

RITA : Oh dear! So what should we do?

DR. IM : We should have happiness and rejoicing and be happy all the time. Do nice things and don't do bad things, and you will have a healthier life. So, walk everyday, smile everyday, be happy everyday, and you get more oxygen.

1 Thessalonians 5:15, 16, 18 says: "See that none render evil for evil unto any man; but ever follow that which is good, both among yourselves, and to all men. Rejoice evermore. … In everything give thanks: for this is the will of God in Christ Jesus concerning you."

This tells us to be in a state of thanksgiving. Being thankful and happy produces endorphins which fight cancer and disease. Anger causes arthritis and causes blood vessels to shrink.

RITA : So, the remedy is…….

DR. IM : The remedy for these diseases, headaches, bone disease, leukemia, and others, is: no bad words, and always pursue good like it says in 1 Thessalonians 5:15.

Also, we should love and pray for our enemies like it says in Matthew 5: 43–48: "Ye have heard that it hath been said, Thou shalt love thy neighbor, and hate thine enemy. But I say unto you, Love your enemies, bless them that curse you, do good to them that hate you, and pray for them which despitefully use you, and persecute you; That ye may be the children of your Father which is in heaven: for he maketh his sun to rise on the evil and on the good, and sendeth rain on the just and on the unjust. For if ye love them which love you, what reward have ye? do not even the publicans the same? And if ye salute your brethren only, what do ye more than others? do not even the publicans so? Be ye therefore perfect, even as your Father which is in heaven is perfect."

When cancer patients repent, they get well.

I have seen five patients with pancreatic cancer get well with prayer and Bible study!

RITA : Oh! WOW!

DR. IM : If I have Jesus' mind, character, and behavior, THEN I can say, "I am a Christian."

The very best healing is to let Jesus live in us. Cancer cannot survive when Jesus lives in us. Over a thousand cases of cancer got well this way.

RITA : Well, that makes sense, because when Jesus comes into our lives, Satan has to leave—he can't stay anymore, so his cancer can't either! I never thought of that before!

DR. IM : A woman came to me—her body had cancer all through it. The doctors had given her two months to live. I showed her these verses about being in a happy state of thanksgiving. She started praying and studying her Bible, and followed the instructions exactly, and in a few weeks, her cancer went away.

RITA : WOW! That's even more than fantastic!

DR. IM : Genesis 1:29, 30 tells us what to eat: "And God said, Behold, I have given you every herb bearing seed, which is upon the face of all the earth, and every tree, in the which is the fruit of a tree yielding seed; to you it shall be for meat. And to every beast of the earth, and to every fowl of the air, and to every thing that creepeth upon the earth, wherein there is life, I have given every green herb for meat: and it was so."

We were made in His image (Genesis 1:27). What IS His image?

RITA : Uh; looks like Him?

DR. IM : Yes, and His image is His way, His conversation. By the food we eat, our character is developed. To the wild animals God gave grass to eat. The lions eat meat—and they are killers. The deer and rabbits obey and eat vegetation, and they are not a threat—they don't kill. Depression comes from eating meat, and we also acquire animal characteristics when we eat their flesh.

RITA : My neighbor and good friend has bone cancer.

DR. IM : Our bones—

(1) support our body weight;

(2) produce our blood hemoglobin and hematocrit, white blood cells, and red blood cells.

The immune system is to protect from viruses, germs, bacteria, and cancer cells. Cancer cells are a virus. There is no antibiotic to kill viruses or cancer cells. Chemotherapy and radiation treatment kills both good cells and bad cells, so, we are dying.

Some doctors advise cancer patients to eat such things as meat, chicken, fish, cheese, butter, and so forth; but cancer cells develop from ALL animal products and animal oil. In the book, *Counsels on Diet and Foods*, page 379, it says that God gave animal products as a curse to ancient Israel. That is why they died in the wilderness.

> *Keeping His commandments is obeying His way. Unkindness, complaining, and anger shut Jesus out from dwelling in me*

Preservatives, color, and chemicals that are put into meat produce cancer cells. Genesis 1:27, 29, 30 says that God gives us a vegetarian diet with no animal products.

Numbers 11:33 says: "And while the flesh was yet between their teeth, ere it was chewed, the wrath of the Lord was kindled against the people, and the LORD smote the people with a very great plague."

RITA : OH, WOW! Yes, it does say that! That's right.

DR. IM : Another important text that explains another part of our human condition that also needs overcoming, is in Matthew 15: 8, 9: "This people draweth nigh unto me with their mouth, and honoreth me with their lips; but their heart is far from me. But in vain they do worship me, teaching for doctrines the commandments of men."

This tells us that people honor God with their lips, but their hearts are far away from heaven and Him. Their worship of God is in vain. What does vain mean?

RITA : Useless?

DR. IM : Yes, their worship is useless. Why did Jesus come the first time?

RITA : To show us how to live?

DR. IM : Yes. And Matthew 9:13 tells us that Jesus came for sinners to repent. Why is He coming back the second time?

RITA : Ummmm …

DR. IM : In Hebrews 9:28, it tells us He comes the second time for those who have quit sinning. "So Christ was once offered to bear the sins of many; and unto them that look for him shall he appear the second time without sin unto salvation."

Matthew 5:48: "Be ye therefore perfect, even as your Father which is in heaven is perfect."

We need to start with our own home by being a good example to our family. Anger disqualifies us for heaven.

1 Thessalonians 5:23, 24 says: "And the very God of peace sanctify you wholly; and I pray God your whole spirit and soul and body be preserved blameless unto the coming of our Lord Jesus Christ. Faithful is he that calleth you, who also will do it."

Our thinking and our ways need to change to be like His ways. We shame Jesus with our anger.

He is waiting for us to repent, "Faithful is he that calleth you, who also will do it." Verse 24. He will do it in us IF we will LET Him.

I am the enemy of Jesus … but He forgives me—so, I SHOULD forgive MY enemies. I get angry, so, I get sick. But if I let Him, Jesus will do it—He will heal me physically and spiritually. What does "repent" mean?

RITA	:	Turn around?
DR. IM	:	Yes—to turn around. No more anger. Love your enemies. When Jesus is in you, what kind of cancer cell can survive?
RITA	:	Well…
DR. IM	:	NONE.
RITA	:	WOW! That is more than fantastic! We SURE serve an *awesome* God—He wants us well!

Dr. Im., please tell us your miracle story.

DR. IM : My wife, Peggy, and I were at a camp meeting in the mountains of Idaho. We were worshipping on Sabbath morning, and I went to help a friend open the heavy iron gate that blocked the road. When we swung the gate open on its hinges, the heavy gate swung back and hit me on the chest, knocking me to the ground, unconscious for three minutes. When I regained consciousness, my doctor friend had called an ambulance, which was not able to get all the way up to the camp. Some of the men helped lift me into my friend's car, and we went half-way down the mountain to meet the ambulance. I was transported to the nearest hospital in Sandpoint, Idaho. Here they did all the X-rays, CAT scans, and an EKG, and told us that the inside of my heart had ruptured from the blow of the heavy iron gate. They could not do the open-heart surgery there to correct it. They would have to send me to the larger hospital in Spokane, Washington. It is more than a two-hour drive by ambulance, and the doctor told us I would need helicopter transport. The doctor at Spokane said, "If you don't come within two hours, you will die."

The Sandpoint Hospital did not have that service, but a helicopter had just flown in with another patient coming to the Sandpoint Hospital, thus God provided it just when it was needed! With the helicopter, it was only a half-hour flight to the larger hospital in Spokane. There were thirty-three cardiac surgeons there, and the one God had picked for me was among the top five. When we landed on the roof of the hospital, the surgeon was already there, and he said to me, "I checked all the X- rays, CAT scan, and EKG. Two layers of your heart are ruptured inside. You need emergency surgery, but you will die whether you have surgery or not, because, with this kind of surgery, I have to open the heart, and the blood will spill out. So, I have a question for you: do you still want to have surgery?"

I said, "I have no answer, so let me pray to God and ask Him, in this situation, if I should have surgery or not."

The doctor said, "Go ahead and ask God first." So, in front of him, out loud, I prayed to the Lord and asked Him, "Shall I have surgery, or not?"

During the prayer, I heard a voice from heaven say, "Do it."

So I said "Thank you, Lord." Then I told the surgeon, "Please do it, because God said so."

Then he took me into surgery, saying that it would take six hours. I said, "OK."

Afterwards, in the recovery room, he came to me. I said, "Thank you, Doctor."

He replied, "Don't thank me. It wasn't me that did it. It was done by heaven. That's why you are still alive."

I said, "Why?"

He said, "I did the same kind of surgery with nine cases before you, and they all died. You are the only one that survived, because God did the surgery on you."

I said, "Thank the Lord." We praised God.

I was discharged after only eight days in the hospital. Normal recovery time for this surgery would have been one-and-a-half to three months. That was four years ago. I am alright, thank God. It has been a total miracle. I am still alive! God bless. This is my story. Please tell this story to everybody, because God loves us!!

RITA : He sure does! God is in everybody's lives if we would only acknowledge Him. Thank you, Dr. Im.

*A special note of appreciation to Mrs. Peggy Im and Mrs. Betty Jo Hadley Jones for their assistance in the orchestrating of this interview.

Miracles Back to Back

One brisk autumn morning here in the North Carolina mountains, I woke up early. Inside the house was cold, in the 40s. Lying in bed, I remembered there was no cut/split wood yet to start a fire. I said a prayer that God would show me how to get the house warm without wood. He brought to my mind that there was a lot of paper and cardboard, so I decided to stuff as much of that paper and cardboard as I could into the stove and light it. By the time it burned up, it would at least knock the chill off in the house. So I got up, made my bed, and walked into the living room to start my cardboard fire. But there in the metal wood box was split wood—just the right size for the wood stove! I was surprised because there was no split wood at my house at all and here was the wood box FULL of split wood! I started a fire with the paper and cardboard AND "real wood" on it. The house got toasty warm.

About an hour later, I heard a big bang and ran back into the living room to see what it was. Part of the hall ceiling had fallen to the floor in all of the high wind we were having outside. That made a three-foot hole in the ceiling which immediately caused the house to start getting cold again because the outside temperature was in the 20s and the high wind was blowing in through the attic.

I got the kitchen stool and tried to put the ceiling pieces back up, but then I broke one, so decided I had better leave them alone. I prayed again that God would show me what to do. Then I tried to call a few people on the telephone, but couldn't reach anyone. Everyone had already gone to work for the day.

I called my friend, Clarence, who does my yard work, but he was working, too, and couldn't come until evening to fix it. So, I guessed I would just have to let it be cold in the house. (Except that I WAS praying that God would do something.)

> *It had to be an angel that put that split wood there for me to get a fire going that morning*

About half an hour later, Clarence showed up at the front door. It turns out that right after we talked on the phone—and I was praying—the people that Clarence was working for decided to cancel for the morning and wanted him to come back in the afternoon. So Clarence had all morning free to fix the hall ceiling. Isn't God *awesome,* how He worked that out!?

While Clarence was working on the ceiling, I thanked him for putting that split wood in the wood box for me to use until the other big logs got split. Clarence looked at me and said, "I didn't bring that wood. I was just gonna ask you where you got it."

No one else had been at my house. Plus, I then remembered that the wood wasn't there the night before and it did not come from my house or property, because there wasn't any there. I remembered thinking when I woke up that morning that there was no wood to start a fire to warm up the house. My house doors were locked all night. So it had to be an angel that put that split wood there for me to get a fire going that morning!

God is so *awesome!* That was two miracles back to back. I said "Thank you" prayers all the rest of that day for the wood and getting the ceiling fixed.

"Blessed be the Lord, who daily loadeth us with benefits" (Ps. 68:19).

A Progressive Thought

One morning, at 4:00 a.m., when I was up praying and studying my Bible, it suddenly hit me—we are now in the time of judgment that the Bible talks about in Revelation 14:7. When this judgment is finished, our probation will be closed.

That means the world is right now on probation. This country is on probation, this state, county, city, ME. I'm on probation right now, and my probation is about to end. It's almost over for the whole world. But we know from the Bible, in 1 Peter 4:17, that judgment for God's people begins first, before the rest of the world.

We are told that, "The present world is designed as a scene of probation for man. He is here to form a character which will pass with him into the eternal world. Good and evil are placed before him, and his future state depends upon the choice he makes. Christ came to change the current of his thoughts and affections. His heart must be removed from his earthly treasure, and placed upon the heavenly. By his self-denial, God can be glorified. The great sacrifice has been made for man. Satan and his angels are combined against the people of God; but Jesus is seeking to purify them unto Himself" (*Testimonies for the Church*, vol. 1, pp. 196, 197).

After this realization hit me, I started examining myself. Have I done, thought, said everything I possibly can to encourage others and myself to be ready? Is there anyone else I need to tell, encourage, enlighten, help toward Jesus? Am I praying for everyone I should be praying for? Am I praying to God for my own salvation? Am I working out my own salvation with fear and trembling, like the Bible tells me in Philippians 2:12? "Wherefore, my beloved, as ye have always obeyed, not as in my presence only, but now much more in my absence, work out your own salvation with fear and trembling."

Jesus wants me—us—to live with Him forever. One illustration you may have heard that has helped me to see this even more clearly is this…

A dad took his two teen boys out in their boat, fishing on the ocean. After a few hours, the two boys tired of fishing and wanted to swim a while. Their dad said, "You can swim right here close to the boat." So, in they jumped, laughing and playing in the cool water around them.

Suddenly, sitting in the boat, their dad saw in the distance a shark fin protruding out of the water. It was coming their way. Their dad yelled a warning, "Boys, get out of the water, quickly, get into the boat!"

The boys said, "Okay, Dad, just a minute."

Again, he said, "Boys, there is a shark! Get back in the boat, NOW!"

"Okay, Dad, we'll finish this game, and get right in."

Frantically, Dad tried to reach out and grab his delaying boys. But they were so engrossed with what THEY were doing, they kept putting off getting out of the water. One last time, their dad yelled, "Boys, PLEASE come into the boat NOW!"

"Yes, Dad, we're coming, just one more minute."

By now, the shark was almost upon them.

Their dad, in desperation, cut his arms, and dove, all bloody into the water, and swam away from the boat, so that the shark would follow him. What more could their dad do to save his boys? He gave his life for them.

Jesus gave His life for us. Jesus has done His part. In fact, He has given His life for the whole world and for you and me. There is nothing else He can do to save us. Have I done my part? Have I accepted Him? Am I living and thinking and talking *everyday* like Him? Or, am I so engrossed with what I am doing, that I keep putting HIM off? I want to be like Jesus. WOW! What a thought!!!

"We are homeward bound. He who loved us so much as to die for us hath builded for us a city. The New Jerusalem is our place of rest. There will be no sadness in the City of God. No wail of sorrow, no dirge of crushed hopes and buried affections, will evermore be heard. Soon the garments of heaviness will be changed for the wedding garment. Soon we shall witness the coronation of our King. Those whose lives have been hidden with Christ, those who on this earth have fought the good fight of faith, will shine forth with the Redeemer's glory in the kingdom of God" (White, *The Adventist Home*, 542.3).

What about yesterday, when I got upset with Millie over—oh dear, what was it over? See, Jesus wouldn't have acted that way. Jesus didn't allow Himself to think of Himself. He never said, "I deserve better than this," or "They can't get away with that." He thought of that person that was beating him, and the one spitting in His face, and He said, "Father, forgive them; for they know not what they do" (Luke 23:34).

No one has ever beat me, spat on me, or killed me. No matter what someone says against me or does to me, it is still not as bad as Jesus went through. I need to think of Jesus standing in that courtroom, taking all of that abuse. They were *falsely* accusing Him—that is SO hard to take, but He did. They spat in His face. YUK! They beat Him. His back was all bloody. They put that crown of thorns on His head and pushed it down into His temples. And, yet, I cry when I get one little splinter in my finger.

If anyone had reason to be mad at someone or have hurt feelings over the way He was treated, Jesus did—but, He didn't allow Himself to even have one thought like we do. If He had had one thought like ours—retaliation or anything—He would not have been our perfect example and sacrifice, and we would all have been lost!

No, I can't be my sinful self anymore. When someone says something derogatory or does not treat me right, I've got to remember that's between them and God; I only need to answer for it IF I have bad feelings toward them. I must pray for them and love them like Jesus does! You can't hate someone you are praying for. I pray that God will save everyone I know. He can do that if we all let Him. Then, if God brings a certain name to my mind, I pray *especially* for that one. Remember, even Jesus, when He was on this earth, prayed to God His Father for us, too—you and me. He prayed, "Father, I will that they also, whom thou hast given me, be with me where I am" (John 17:24). You may read Jesus' whole prayer for us in John 17:1–26.

Dear Reader, won't it be super great, if when you get to heaven, everyone you ever knew on this earth is there, because YOU prayed for them?! After all, I want to be like Jesus. He will help me if I ask Him to, and if I let Him. And He will help you, too, if you let Him.

"He that overcometh shall inherit all things; and I will be his God, and he shall be my son [daughter]" (Rev. 21:7).

Love Divine, All Loves Excelling

1. Love divine, all loves excelling, Joy of heaven to earth come down,
fix in us thy humble dwelling, all thy faithful mercies crown.
Jesus, thou art all compassion, pure, unbounded love thou art;
visit us with thy salvation, enter every trembling heart.

2. Breathe, O breathe thy loving Spirit into every troubled breast;
let us all in thee inherit, let us find the promised rest.
Take away the love of sinning, Alpha and Omega be;
end of faith, as its beginning, set our hearts at liberty.

3. Come, almighty to deliver, let us all thy life receive;
suddenly return, and never, nevermore thy temples leave.
Thee we would be always blessing, serve thee as thy hosts above,
pray and praise thee without ceasing, glory in thy perfect love.

4. Finish then thy new creation, pure and spotless let us be;
let us see thy great salvation perfectly restored in thee:
changed from glory into glory, till in heaven we take our place,
till we cast our crowns before thee, lost in wonder, love, and praise.

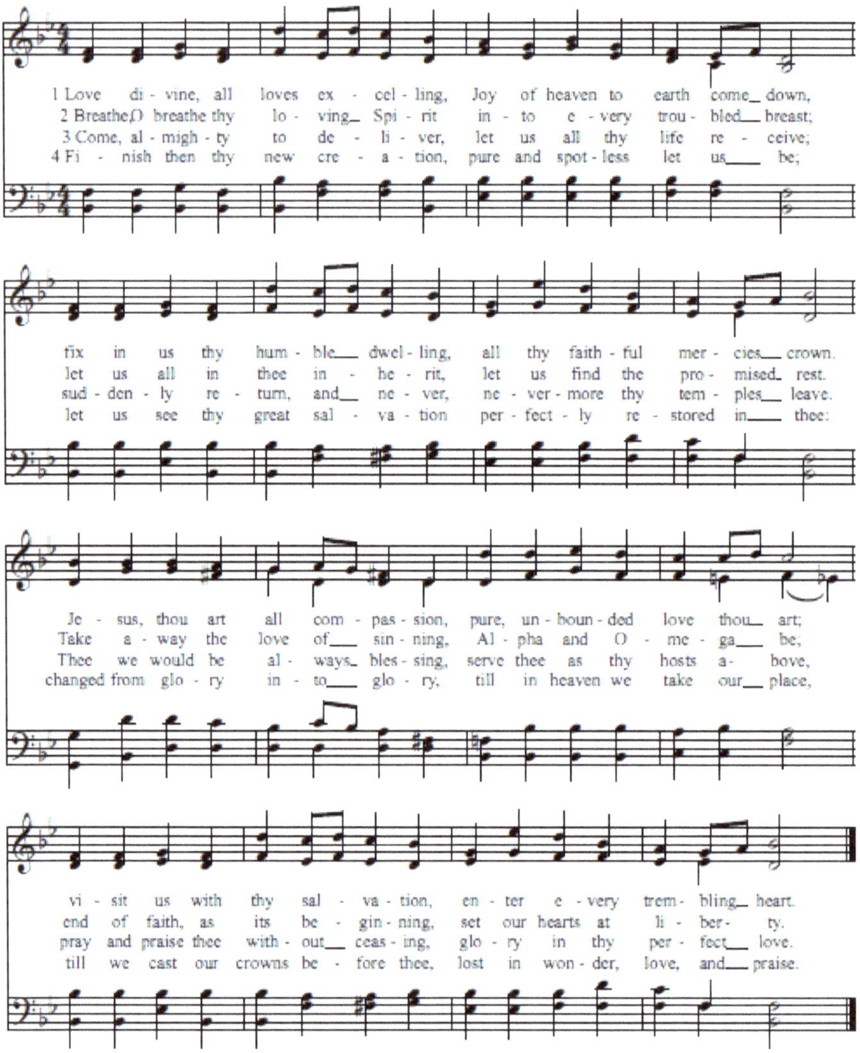

Text: Charles Wesley (1707-1788)
Tune: John Zundel (1815-1882)

87 87D
BEECHER

Epilogue

Thankfully God IS in MY life, and God IS in YOUR life. Remember that, and keep looking to HIM.

Those whom the Lamb [Jesus] shall lead by the fountains of living waters, [Revelation 7:17] and from whose eyes he shall wipe away all tears [Revelation 21:4] will be those NOW receiving the knowledge and understanding revealed in the Bible, the Word of God. To us has been given the privilege of receiving the wisdom that cometh from God, of seeing the beauty and the glories of that Word which lies at the foundation of all true knowledge. The Bible teaches us what a Christian ought to be, and what he ought to do.

"We are to copy NO HUMAN BEING. There is no human being wise enough to be our criterion. We are to look to the man Christ Jesus, who is complete in the perfection of righteousness and holiness. He is the author and finisher of our faith. He is the pattern Man. His experience is the measure of the experience that we are to gain. His character is our model. Let us, then, take our minds OFF the perplexities and the difficulties of this life, and fix them on HIM, that by beholding we may be changed into HIS LIKENESS. We may behold Christ to good purpose. We may safely look to him; for he is all-wise. As we look to him and think of him, he will be formed within [our hearts], the hope of glory.

"Let us strive with all the power that God has given us to be among the hundred and forty-four thousand [Revelation 7:1–8]. And let us do all that we can to help others to gain heaven."

—E.G. White, *Review and Herald*, March 9, 1905.

TEACH Services, Inc.
PUBLISHING

We invite you to view the complete
selection of titles we publish at:
www.TEACHServices.com

We encourage you to write us
with your thoughts about this,
or any other book we publish at:
info@TEACHServices.com

TEACH Services' titles may be purchased in
bulk quantities for educational, fund-raising,
business, or promotional use.
bulksales@TEACHServices.com

Finally, if you are interested in seeing
your own book in print, please contact us at:
publishing@TEACHServices.com

We are happy to review your manuscript at no charge.

www.ingramcontent.com/pod-product-compliance
Lightning Source LLC
Chambersburg PA
CBHW040315170426
43196CB00020B/2936